Living Below Your Means

Living Below Your Means: A Practical Guide to Financial Freedom

Jennifer Raschig

Copyright Information

First Printing: 2020

Print edition ISBN: 9781658705103

Raschig Creative Works

W2190 Turner Rd

Jefferson, WI 53549

www.jenniferraschig.com

Acknowledgements

Thank you to my clients for trusting me with your financial future. Your questions about information I provided in my first book have helped to make this second edition so much better.

I would be remiss if I didn't also acknowledge the readers of my first book, too. You took a chance on a new author and I'm very appreciative!

As always, many thanks to my family for being the sounding board and helpful editors for my projects. I love you all!

Table of Contents

A Note to My Readers

When I set out to write the first edition (Living Within Your Means: A practical guide to financial freedom) of this book, I had one thing in mind: Help you get out of debt and onto the road of a more secure financial future by understanding where your money is going and making practical decisions about how to spend it.

Here I am, 2 years later, updating the book. You may be wondering what advice has changed so significantly in the last two years that I needed to publish a new version. Well, the original advice is still sound, and I stand by it. However, some of the tools and resources I list in the first edition are no longer available, or something better now exists. Also, I felt like the first edition was a bit incomplete.

With the updated guide, you're going to get more about "what's next." If you've been really successful in making the changes you need to live beneath your means, you're most likely going to be inspired to continue to make changes so that you can truly be financially independent. This updated guide gets you going on that path, with a bonus section on achieving the next level of financial freedom. Thank you for reading and I hope you enjoy. I would love to hear your feedback! You can contact me and find more about this book or other creative works at www.jenniferraschig.com!

Jennifer Raschig

Preface

Peter and Katie

Katie had trouble holding down a job for more than a year. There was always something that prevented her from staying - either she got fired, or she decided that the work was too hard or boring. Plus, Katie often wanted "things" to show for her hard work. She would spontaneously purchase new cell phones, clothing, or the newest fitness device to reward herself for working. At one point, Katie decided that to do what she really wanted to do, she had to go back to school to earn her degree. However, she couldn't possibly work at the same time. She was never very good at focusing on more than one thing at a time.

Peter, Katie's husband, had a steady job that paid less than $50,000 a year. The work wasn't terribly interesting, but he knew he had to stick with it. Being a bit more realistic about their financial situation, he tried to cut corners where he could. He had a hard time telling Katie that they really couldn't afford all the stuff she was buying. He wanted to see her happy. Besides, he thought if he let her buy some things, she'd be more willing to help cut out other nonessential items to save money.

Peter eventually took on a second job to make ends meet. Still, with only Peter working and Katie not cutting her spending at all, their debt skyrocketed and overwhelmed them. While they were making most of their minimum payments on their credit cards, sometimes they missed a month on one so they could pay another that seemed more urgent. Peter handled paying the bills. He told Katie that their spending had to stop. Katie's solution was to file bankruptcy. She felt like they would never get out of the vicious cycle otherwise. Of course, Peter argued that they wouldn't be in this situation if Katie could just stop spending money and go back to work. But just as he could not tell Katie no when she wanted to buy things, he eventually gave in to the bankruptcy.

After the bankruptcy was granted, Peter and Katie only had their mortgage payment and their car payment. After paying those, they had quite a bit leftover that had previously gone to credit cards. Katie caught on to that quickly and started buying again. This time, they weren't going in to debt because creditors wouldn't give them any credit, but they weren't getting ahead either.

Does this sound familiar? Unfortunately, it does for far too many people. I hope you picked this book up before you got to the point of bankruptcy and no credit - but if not, that's ok. This book is meant to give you hope, to help you dig out of the hole and eventually get ahead.

Jennifer Raschig

What is Living Within Your Means?

Introduction

To be successful with this guide, you need to understand what the concept of "living within your means" truly requires. In essence, living within your means is creating a lifestyle that allows you to, at the very least, have your needs met without going into debt. In basic terms, you can live on the money coming in to your bank account every month. When you think about that concept, what do you need to do differently to accomplish it? If you follow this guide, in the end, you could be living debt-free and maybe even pulling ahead.

The key, of course, is being able to follow the guide. If you are married, or in a relationship and you share financial resources, you must follow this guide as a team. Ultimately, if you and your partner are not on the same financial terms, you will have conflict when trying to carry out many of the tasks outlined in these pages. To put this in perspective - if you go out and buy a $1200 computer and don't consult your partner, will they be upset? If the answer is anything other than "no," you will have conflict.

If you haven't pulled them in already, now is the time. Talk to them about this book and how you are trying to improve your lives together and the need for them to be involved. You may meet some resistance. Finances are frequently a touchy subject. If you think you might have some difficulty in approaching your partner about this, try taking the stance of planning for your future together.

Painting a picture of a bright future puts a positive spin on what you're trying to do (and it _is_ beneficial for your relationship)! Then, let your partner know how the current money situation makes you feel. If you're feeling weighed down or depressed, it's affecting most aspects of your life.

But, don't blame! That's a surefire way of shutting down the conversation for a very long time. Use "I" rather than "you." For example, say, "I feel so sad when I can't see the light at the end of the tunnel, and I worry about our future."

If you don't take the time to work through the resistance, you may not be able to implement some of the changes recommended. Your partner may feel hurt, resentful, or angry if you begin cutting expenses in areas they aren't comfortable with without their input. This is an important point and you need to take sufficient time to ensure your partner is on board.

Needs vs. Wants

When we break down the concept of living within your means, we're left with two major components: 1. Have your needs met, and 2. Don't go into debt. While some debt may not be considered "bad," when you are learning to live only on the income you currently have, you will get in the habit of spending money only on something you could pay cash for.

"Needs" can mean different things to different people. My definition is housing, food, and sufficient transportation. Within each of those categories are individual items that we would most likely consider a necessity. Take housing, for example. Whether you live in an apartment, condo, or house, there are certain other expenses that go along with that. Utilities, such as electricity and water, and insurance are a couple examples of other expenses associated with your residence.

Some things, like meeting obligations of already existing debt, may seem like a need - and in the long run, your financial situation will be much better and easier to navigate if you meet that commitment. However, you can LIVE without paying that debt if you had to. Your definition of a need may be different, and that's ok. But keep my definition in mind as you move through the exercises.

In the fast-paced society we live in, where information is immediately available, we get accustomed to having what we want, when we want it - usually right now. It's sometimes difficult to delay purchasing, especially if we have a credit card with an available balance. The advent of online shopping with fast shipping only feeds the spending monster inside some of us. We must train ourselves to resist immediate gratification. This may be the hardest part of living within your means. You may slip up occasionally as you move toward financial freedom. Don't let that stop you from your goal. Acknowledge your mistake and get back on track.

When considering a purchase, think about the categories of needs or wants and where this item or service fits in. Is it something you can physically live without? Some people use the trick of delaying the purchase for a week. Does it still seem like something you must have? What purpose will it serve, or what need will it fill? Get in the habit of asking these questions before making any purchase that isn't in your already defined "needs" list. This is tough. I get it. You can start a list of wants that you can't afford now.

Eventually, as you save up and can keep up with your needs, you can begin to purchase items from your wants list.

Debt Discussion

The second part of the equation is to avoid going into debt. Some people believe that specific kinds of debt are okay. Think of your mortgage, for example. You might think this is "good" debt. There are even some popular financial advisors who prefer you to keep mortgage debt because, depending on your interest rate on your mortgage, you'd get a higher return investing that money, rather than paying off your mortgage. Of course, you have to be aware of those interest rates and be sure that your paying less interest on your mortgage than you are gaining in your investments, for that to pan out. Also, you may get a tax deduction for your mortgage interest if you itemize deductions (which fewer people are doing now that the standard deduction amounts have changed).

Each situation is going to be different. But think about this. Would it be worth paying off your mortgage if you didn't have to pay the mortgage every month or keep tabs on all your interest rates? Is that better than potentially getting a tax deduction? In the grand scheme of things, if you must have debt, mortgage debt isn't horrible. However, for many people, having no debt is the ultimate goal.

When referring to debt, there are two main types - secured debt and unsecured. Secured debt is debt that has some sort of collateral that "secures" the bank's interest in the loan. This means that if you don't keep up with the payment, the bank can take the collateral. Usually, this is a mortgage or auto loan. Purchases related to secured debt are often considered necessities. But, let's reserve that thinking for when we do our assessment of what's truly needed to live. Can you "live" without a car? This probably depends on your situation. If you live in a city with reliable, inexpensive public transportation, a car may be an easy purchase to forgo. For those who live in suburban or rural areas, a car may be a necessity. Now, if the secured debt is related to a purchase like an RV or a boat, this is obviously not a "need" (unless you are going to live in it). You can certainly live without either of those items. When you get to the Needs and Wants list, you'll need to be brutally honest with yourself on what you can do without.

Unsecured debts are student loans, personal loans (such as pay-day loans) or credit card debt. Let's talk about credit card or "revolving credit" accounts. This could be a standard credit card or a store card. You probably already have some existing debt on these cards. As you work through establishing a financial plan to live within your current income, a key component will be not adding to this revolving debt. Living solely on your current income means that you won't need to use credit cards routinely for purchases. You will generally be operating on a cash-only basis. This is a huge change for many of us. Plastic is so convenient! Not to mention the ability to use our smart phones as payment methods. Many people don't carry cash of any sort. However, until you get in the habit of only spending what is available from your income, you will need to revert to the days of only spending actual cash you have in your pocket. Honestly, some people MUST only use cash as the lure of the credit card is too strong to resist.

As you control your spending, there could be room to use a credit card for the rewards it offers. You need to be at a point that you can resist overspending and always pay off the entire balance every month. In later chapters, we'll explore options to help you control your plastic habit. Specifically, the Planning Tools chapter will give you many ideas to use.

Practical Application

Think about what your definition of a "need" is. Is it broader than the definition that I gave? If so, why? Use the Beginning Journey Monthly Expense List (Worksheet #1) at the end of the book to make a list of expenses (with associated dollar amount) categorized into needs or wants. These should just be your recurring, monthly expenses at this point. For example, don't include an expense related to buying your niece a birthday gift, because you don't do that every month. You do need to think about things you pay for only yearly, such as property tax, too. If you need help remembering those annual expenses, pull out credit card or bank statements to catch those. Divide the yearly expense by 12 to get the monthly amount and add it to your list. Go ahead and do that now. You need that list to move on. Again, if you share the financial responsibilities, complete the worksheet with your partner. By the way, you might want to think about either printing several copies of the worksheet or doing this exercise in pencil. You will be making a lot of revisions. By the way, all the worksheets listed in this book are also available on www.jenniferraschig.com/books.

On the Money Coming In (Worksheet #2), list all sources of current income. This income can be from your current job(s), social security income, child support, etc. List those sources of income that you can count on routinely. Do not list the occasional $50 you get for helping a friend out. Enter the amount you get after all taxes and other deductions are taken out, or the "net" amount. Also add any income from investments, such as interest income that you routinely receive.

Once you have your income documented, compare money coming in to the "Needs" list. Is there enough cash coming in to cover your needs? If not, review your expenses again. What else can you cut? In later chapters, we'll review how to reduce those necessary expenses or create extra income. For now, we just need to see what the gap is.

Case Study

Remember Peter and Katie from the beginning of this book? (Hint: if you didn't read the Preface, you'll find them there). Peter has a sister named Becky. She talked with Peter a few times about his and Katie's financial situation. The conversations made her realize that she needed to look at how she and her husband were living.

Becky is a 30-year-old administrative assistant, married with 2 children. Kyle, her husband, works on the production line in a local factory. He's not thrilled with his job, but without an education beyond high school, he doesn't feel like he has too many options to do something different. They live in the Midwest in a suburban area. Becky has decided that she wants to take control of her family's financial situation as they keep getting deeper in debt, living paycheck to paycheck.

Becky made a list of expenses that she and Kyle have every month. The unexpected expenses, generally, were being paid with a credit card. They weren't true monthly expenses. She'd eventually like to have an emergency fund for those things, but she wasn't sure how to make that happen. For now, Becky just wanted to understand if they could live on their current income.

After Becky made the list, she realized her "needs" list was significantly longer than her wants. She had the monthly fee for her son's soccer league in the Needs column. She also had her monthly salon visit, which included an expense for a manicure every month. Kyle was in a bowling league and that added up to about $150 a month. Along with those expenses, Becky listed the internet, cable and cell phone bills. The list below shows Becky's original Beginning Journey Monthly Expense list.

Living Below Your Means

Needs	$ Amount	Wants	$ Amount
Mortgage	1500	Clothing/Shoes	100
Electric bill	175	College Savings	100
Gas bill	75	Gym	50
Cell phone	200		
Groceries /Dining Out	800		
Cable/Internet	150		
Visa card	100		
Discover	60		
Target store card	30		
Home insurance	80		
Car payments	650		
Car insurance	125		
Gasoline	360		
Medical/Dental insurance	600		
Soccer league	25		
Bowling league	150		
Salon	125		
Total Needs	**$5205**	**Total Wants**	**$250**

Then, Becky tackled the monthly income. She and Kyle only had paychecks from their jobs. Neither had a second job or any other income to consider. Once Becky completed the Money Coming In worksheet, it looked like this.

Worksheet #2

Source	$ Amount
Becky's income	2700
Kyle's income	2340
Total Income	**$5040**
Subtract $ amount of Total Needs (from Worksheet 1)	-$5205
Total Extra $ or Gap	**-$165**

Wow! What a gap. According to how she had the expenses listed, her family was almost $200 short of the being able to pay for what she considered as basic needs. No wonder they were putting so much on their credit cards every month! Her first thought was that she was going to have to tell Kyle that he could no longer be in the bowling league. And, on top of that she was going to have to reduce her visits to the salon and only go every other month. That would cut that expense in half. But she still thought of the salon visit as a necessity.

When Kyle got home from work, Becky sprang the news - no more bowling because there just wasn't money, and it wasn't a necessary expense. As you can imagine, Kyle was furious! He had no idea Becky had started looking at their budget. She had never discussed this with him. On top of that, she made the decision on what to cut without talking to him. Becky's progress on taking control of their finances was halted.

A few days later, Kyle had calmed down. Although he was still frustrated that Becky made decisions without him, he realized the need and importance of getting their finances on track. He and Becky sat down together to review her list of Needs and Wants. Together, they revised it to what their actual needs were and realized they had enough to cover those needs and some of their wants. They agreed they would set some time aside the following weekend to discuss which items on their wants list they would continue to pay for monthly.

Worksheet #1

Needs	$ Amount	Wants	$ Amount
Mortgage	1500	Clothing/Shoes	100
Electric bill	175	College Savings	100
Gas bill	75	Gym	50
Cell phone	200	Soccer league	25
Groceries /Dining Out	800	Bowling league	150
Cable/Internet	150	Salon	125
Visa card	100		
Discover	60		
Target store card	30		
Home insurance	80		
Car payments	650		
Car insurance	125		
Gasoline	360		
Medical/Dental insurance	600		
Total Needs	**$4905**	**Total Wants**	**$550**

Even with this revised list, Becky and Kyle realize that they probably have some items listed as needs that may not fit in that category. However, their revised Money Coming In worksheet shows a better picture of being able to provide for their needs.

Living Below Your Means

Worksheet #2

Source	$ Amount
Becky's income	2700
Kyle's income	2340
Total Income	**$5040**
Subtract $ amount of Total Needs (from Worksheet 1)	-$4905
Total Extra $ or Gap	**$135**

Whittling down the necessary expenses

Although you may have done a good job of organizing the major categories of your expenses as wants or needs, you might have some individual items that could be pulled out as a want. Let's look at your list a little closer. Are there expenses related to entertainment in the "needs" category? An example might be your cable bill. Is this truly necessary? Would you be able to live without cable television? While you may be thinking that you couldn't possibly go without it, in reality, cable is a luxury (and there are many alternatives). With that in mind, go through the list once more and re-categorize those into "wants."

Next, look at salon services or other beauty items, such as haircuts and coloring, makeup purchases, waxing... you get the idea. Again, as much as we love to look good, these things aren't necessary to live.

Another category that we need to look at is groceries and dining out. Becky listed this as one item. She and Kyle would need to separate those as they should be treated differently. Groceries are a necessity (and we'll learn some strategies to save money on groceries, too). Dining out is not. Estimate approximately how much you spend per month on eating out and move that amount to the "wants" list. Later, we'll use some tools to get more specific numbers to plug in.

While many people list credit card payments as a need, they definitely aren't needed to live. Yes, you have created an obligation to pay, and we'll get into strategies to meet that commitment if there really isn't enough to pay that debt. But these expenses should be in the wants list. Paying your credit card isn't needed to survive.

Keep doing this review of the needs list until you're very sure you have only absolute needs in that column. Now, enter the total dollar amount of the needs at the bottom of the list. Then subtract the "needs" amount from the total monthly income. If there is still a gap, don't worry! We will go over some additional tools and strategies to reduce some of those truly necessary expenses.

Decide on the extras

If you have extra income over your absolute needs, decide which items you will be able to afford on your wants list. If you have extra income beyond your absolute needs and have credit card debt, you should plan on including the minimum payments in your budget. (You'll be creating a budget in the next chapter).

Becky and Kyle did this exercise, too. Because they had enough to pay their credit card payments, they left that on their Needs list, but did move "Dining Out" over to the Wants side. She also moved the "Cable/Internet" item to the wants side. Their third revision of Worksheet 1 looked like this:

Jennifer Raschig

Worksheet #1

Needs	$ Amount	Wants	$ Amount
Mortgage	1500	Clothing/Shoes	100
Electric bill	175	College Savings	100
Gas bill	75	Gym	50
Cell phone	200	Dining Out	100
Groceries	700	Cable/Internet	150
Visa card	100	Soccer league	25
Discover	60	Bowling league	150
Target store card	30	Salon	125
Home insurance	80		
Car payments	650		
Car insurance	125		
Gasoline	360		
Medical/Dental insurance	600		
Total Needs	**$4655**	**Total Wants**	**$800**

Beyond obligations that affect your credit report, try to keep the wants to a minimum. In the long run, you want to be able to plan for the future. If every single dollar is spent today, you won't be able to make long-term plans.

Summary

To successfully begin living within your means:

- Have a conversation with your partner to get them involved.
- Make a list of your needs and wants - be honest (with yourself and your partner) about what your needs are.
- Revise that list after considering what is absolutely necessary to live - food, housing, and transportation to work or school.
- Make a commitment to not incur any new debt.
- Determine your gap (if any) between cash coming in and cash going out.

Jennifer Raschig

Planning Tools

Introduction

To get you from creating your wants and needs list to actually getting ahead, you need to start budgeting and keeping track of your real expenses. There are so many tools available. You can purchase very sophisticated computer software or apps for your smart phone. Or, you can budget and track manually with the simplest of tools - pencil and paper. No matter which method you decide to use, I can't stress enough the importance of budgeting. To be successful in creating a real budget, you must first track how much money you spend every month and how much is being spent for each specific item.

Knowing where your money is going is the first step. The only way to know that is to do the work. This is painstaking, but I know you can do it! Too many people give up at this point, or only do it half-heartedly. They are left with too many unknowns. They will never figure out exactly how much can be put towards what is absolutely necessary and how to prioritize the items on their "wants" list.

Keep in mind, you may not have to track every single dollar forever. That part of the tracking can be somewhat temporary. It really depends on how disciplined you can be with your spending and how variable your expenses are from month to month.

Doing it Old School

What does "doing it old school" mean? In this case, I'm referring to tracking your expenses and creating a budget without software or an app designed specifically for that purpose. If you have no intention of doing this without budgeting or expense tracking software of some sort, then go ahead and skip to the Software and Apps section.

Let's start with the most basic tools - pencil and paper. You'll need a regular 8 1/2 x 11 lined notebook, a pencil, and a calculator (for those who don't enjoy adding and subtracting without it). Alternatively, if you didn't want to use a notebook, you can use the Budget Planned Vs Actual table (Worksheet #3) at the end of the book.

Start with creating a preliminary budget. Keep in mind this budget is a first draft. You won't be able to establish your final budget until you know where your money is going and how much you actually spend (versus how much you *think* you spend) on things like groceries.

At the top of the first page, write Budget. On each line down the left side, write the items that are on your needs list. Then, write any items that you decided that you had enough income for from your wants list. Next to each item, write the amount you plan to spend on the item that month. For expenses that are variable, you can either choose to use your average monthly expense, or the maximum that the expense would be.

Now, you'll also want to create a column for your actual expenses (see Illustration 1). At the end of the month, we'll total up all receipts and bills for each item and that will be the total of your actual expense for that budget item.

Illustration 1

```
                    JANUARY
                    BUDGET

 PLANNED                        ACTUAL

 MORTGAGE            1500
 HOME INSURANCE        65
 CAR PAYMENT          450
 CAR INSURANCE        100
 GASOLINE             300
 ELECTRIC BILL        150
 GAS BILL              75
 GROCERIES            650
 INTERNET             100
 CELL PHONE           150
 VISA CARD             75
 MEDICAL INSURANCE    400
                   _____
                   $ 4015
```

Creating the draft budget is the easy part. The harder part is keeping track of your actual expenses. When I say keep track of your actual expenses, I do mean <u>every single thing</u> you spend money on. This means if you spend $1.50 at McDonald's for coffee, you need to ask for a receipt and record that expense. Keep an envelope in your car or your purse for receipts so they go in one place while you're out and about. Then, when you get home, place the receipts in a designated folder.

You should also add to the folder any billing statements for bills that you pay, or your check book with the duplicate check showing the amount paid. Place anything in the folder that shows the actual amount that you paid, if you didn't get a receipt for that payment. To be even more organized, you can get an expandable file folder and create labels that match the categories of items in your budget. This will save time when you are totaling your real expenses for each item.

To keep the time spent on tracking manageable, you may need to set aside time every night (or at least weekly) to write down your expenses. If you don't, you're going to spend several hours working on it at the end of the month. This is much harder as your receipts might not be as descriptive as you need them to be for tracking.

You might want to devote an entire notebook page for larger categories, or those that would have multiple entries per month. This would apply to groups like groceries and gasoline. Keep a running total so you know exactly how much you've spent and what is left for that category. (See Illustration 2).

Illustration 2

Groceries

10/9	172.06
10/18	35.22
	207.28
10/24	103.74
	311.02

If a receipt has items that fit into multiple groups, then you should record the actual amount for each category - rather than just recording the receipt amount. For example, you may shop at a warehouse store, like Sam's Club or Costco, where you purchased grocery items and products for your home. You would total only the amount spent on grocery products and record that amount on the notebook page for groceries. Then, you would total the amount for household items and record that under its own category. By the way, in a later chapter, we'll address how you can be even more specific with tracking grocery items and how to save on those purchases.

The first month or two of tracking will be a bit of an eye opener for you. You are probably spending much more in some areas than you really thought. You might need to adjust the planned budget amount, or better yet, find ways to cut back on those expenses (we'll discuss that in a later chapter).

You also will find that you have purchases that don't fit into any of your identified groups. Resist the urge to create a "miscellaneous" group. If you do, it will become a black hole for your cash. It would be too easy to hide purchases that aren't necessary in this grouping. You won't really know where your money has gone. Instead, identify distinct categories that you can group items in. If you just can't figure out how to group those miscellaneous items, list them separately on a page in the notebook. You will keep an eye on the miscellaneous page for the next couple of months. Do you have routine expenses here? Perhaps they are related to entertainment or hobbies? If so, you'll want to create that category and add it to your budget or cut out the expense (see Illustration 3).

Illustration 3

	JANUARY BUDGET	
PLANNED		ACTUAL
MORTGAGE	1500	1500
HOME INSURANCE	65	65
CAR PAYMENT	450	450
CAR INSURANCE	100	100
GASOLINE	300	287
ELECTRIC BILL	150	154
GAS BILL	75	80
GROCERIES	650	670
INTERNET	100	100
CELL PHONE	150	150
VISA CARD	75	73
MEDICAL INSURANCE	400	400
		52 HOBBIES/ENTERTAINMENT
	$ 4015	$4079
		- 4015
		$64 OVER BUDGET

Another "manual" way to keep track is to keep cash in separate envelopes for purchases other than bills you get in the mail. At the beginning of the month, you would take the entire cash amount out of your bank account for each category. For an item like gasoline, you would put your entire budget amount in an envelope labeled "gasoline." Each time you need to fill up, you use only the cash in that envelope. As the month goes on, you'll need to be mindful of the cash left in the envelope. Once it's gone, you don't fill up the tank anymore.

This might remind you of your high school or college days, where every dollar counts - and you might end up putting only $5 in the tank. That's ok! You might also get creative in how you get where you need to be. Can you carpool? Do you truly need to go out? Can you consolidate trips so that you aren't adding unnecessary miles? All of these things will help you stay on budget. And, with the envelope method, it is much less likely that you will go over budget for any item.

You could also modify the envelope method to do 1 or 2 weeks at a time. If you are currently living paycheck to paycheck, taking $300 out of your bank account at the beginning of the month may not work for you. Whatever works for your current income schedule will be fine, as long as the total amount that goes into the envelope in the month is equal to the budgeted dollar amount for that group for that month.

Software and Apps

There are a ton of free apps, paid apps and computer software available for use in 2020. Please keep in mind this book does not endorse use of any one product over another. You will have to decide what works best for you. One word of advice - if you are already struggling to make ends meet, it does not make sense to spend any money on an app or special software to help you.

Spreadsheet programs are one option to consider. You may already have a spreadsheet program on your computer, like Microsoft Excel. You can also use Google Docs for free. Create or sign in to your Google account at www.google.com. From the toolbar, select Docs and then select Sheets (see Illustration 4).

Whether you use Google or Microsoft, or some other spreadsheet program, using this kind of software is relatively easy. Most spreadsheet programs have templates setup already for monthly budgets. You can certainly use a template and modify it to fit what you need. Google Sheets has a monthly budget template that is very easy to use. Microsoft Excel has several templates for budgeting available. Unlike the Google Sheets template, they don't necessarily come with instructions (see Illustration 5). However, once you figure out how to enter your information, the available features in the templates make it very easy to see how closely you've adhered to budget.

Illustration 4

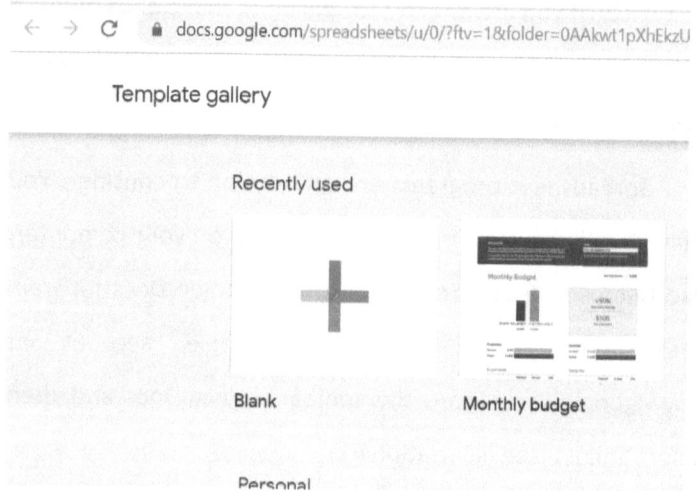

Illustration 5

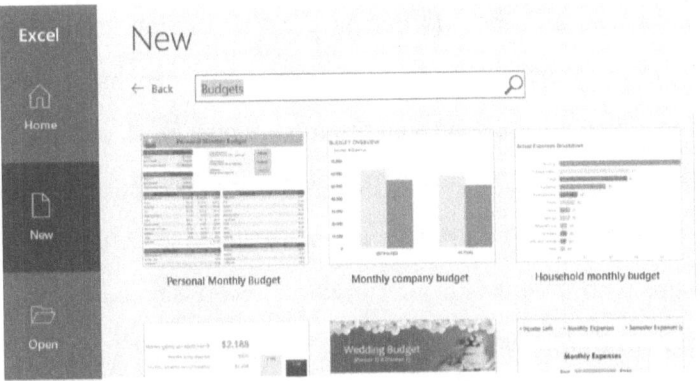

Used with permission from Microsoft

If you don't want to use one of the spreadsheet templates, you can just create the budget and expense tracking yourself. You could set up one sheet in the spreadsheet to be the monthly budget and then track individual expenses on other tabs in the workbook. The tabs in the spreadsheet would be equivalent to the notebook pages discussed in the Doing It Old School section. The biggest difference is that you can use the spreadsheet to do the calculating for you. It's much easier to update the numbers on the spreadsheet, rather than on paper.

There are other computer software applications you can use. A very popular program is Quicken. Quicken is considered a personal finance management software application. This program has much more than just budgeting, and they do not have a free version at all. The Quicken Starter Edition© is the least expensive and depending on your financial situation, it may be all you need. The nice feature with this software is that it will automatically categorize your transactions. So, it definitely helps with the painstaking tracking of every single receipt It has some great reporting tools to help you stay on track, too. Unlike some other options, it doesn't automatically pull from your accounts. You have to trigger the update - but that's as easy as hitting a button. There is a bit of a learning curve, but if you can master it, the software is very powerful.

Another option is YNAB, which stands for You Need a Budget. As of the time of the writing of this book, it is $84 a year and is an online software that helps you create a "job" for every dollar. This really helps you with the tracking of every single dollar that comes in. While the software itself takes some time to learn, it is a good option. It truly is just a budgeting program. It does allow syncing with your accounts, so you will not have to enter all transactions manually. Anything that you buy with cash will still need to be entered to provide a true picture of where your money is going. The nice thing about YNAB is that it has quite a bit of education available to its subscribers. The app also has a forum available so you can get help and support from other users. Having access to a community of others going through similar circumstances will go a long way to helping you stay on track. If you like the idea of education and support along with a very good budgeting software, then YNAB might be the app for you. As long as you can afford it, of course.

Intuit's Mint© is a totally free online software that you connect your various bank and credit card accounts to. It analyzes your spending based on your past transactions and automatically tracks transactions you make in those accounts. The main categories that are available to track your spending are not editable, but you can create subcategories. Just like with all of the software options, you'll still have to enter cash transactions. Still, the analysis that the software does, and the automatic categorization of your transactions is excellent - and you can't beat the price! Mint's reporting features are okay - not nearly as nice as Quicken's. Mint does have an app for your phone, which is also free. You might want to go with Mint if you eventually plan on investing - as you are able to track investments with the app. It's not the best option for that, but it is good enough for those who use a "set it and forget it" investing strategy.

Another software with a phone app to consider is EveryDollar. EveryDollar is newer than Mint, but the programs are similar. Setting up your budget in EveryDollar is very easy. Similar to YNAB, the concept is to show where every single dollar is going. Unfortunately, you can't link your credit card or bank accounts unless you pay for EveryDollar Plus©. This version is $99 at the time of this writing. If you want to stick to the free version, you'll be entering every single transaction in the software. That might not be a bad thing - you'll find out quickly just how often you're spending money and may get really tired of entering all those transactions. The flip side, of course, is that you'll get tired of entering the transactions and just stop tracking altogether. For that reason, I do not recommend the free version of this software.

Case Study

We left Becky and Kyle after they created their Wants vs Needs list. They agreed on where they thought their money should go. Now, they needed to track exactly where money was going now so that they could be sure to stay on track. Kyle noted that he did not want to track expenses manually. If he had to spend more than 5-10 minutes a day on this, he wouldn't keep it up. Becky thought it would be a good idea to have something that links their bank and credit card accounts so that it would cut down on entry of those transactions. That eliminated some of the apps she found when searching online. She and Kyle also agreed that if they could find an app that didn't cost anything, that would be ideal. They didn't want to add to their monthly expenses or cut anything out of their "wants" to finance a way to track their spending. After reviewing their options, Becky and Kyle agreed to use Intuit's Mint®.

That evening, Becky created a Mint® account and spent a few hours creating the subcategories to track their spending. She shared this with Kyle so that they were categorizing expenses in the same way. She also connected all their bank and credit card accounts and she and Kyle both installed the phone app. Becky didn't put too many dollar amounts in the budget yet - she wanted to understand the true cash inflow and outflow before putting something in writing. The only entries that she put an amount in were for predictable expenses like their mortgage and car payments.

One last decision that she and Kyle made before calling it a night was to get and save receipts for every purchase - whether that was a soda and chips from a convenience store, or an online purchase. This way they could make sure that all cash transactions were being added to Mint® and they could talk about the receipts to make sure they were both categorizing the expenses the same.

Setting the accounts up was a lot of work and took much longer than Becky anticipated, but she knew it would be worth it. She already felt better about their finances and that they had started a plan.

Summary

After you've identified your wants and needs, it's time to start tracking your spending to see where your money is going. You can do this through manual tracking or through one of many software applications.

The pros of manual tracking are that it's free and you can do it anywhere - no special equipment needed. Of course, the cons are that it's time consuming and can be error-prone (depending on how good you are at math!).

Software is nice because it's much easier to track spending, and depending on which application you choose, you could have access to some nice reporting features and other education resources. The downside is that it is reliant on needing, at a minimum, an electronic device to access the software, and often an internet connection to sync transactions. And, not all software is free.

The choice is yours, but you need to track where every single dollar you have coming in is going. Decide on a method today and get started setting it up before moving on to the next section.

Jennifer Raschig

The Budget

Introduction

You may think you've got your budget nailed down already since you've learned how to identify your wants vs. your needs, and you've started tracking where your money is going - and maybe even setup a preliminary budget. Well, you're part of the way there. You've made a lot of decisions to this point, but the heavy lifting is about to begin. In this chapter, you'll learn how to take budgeting to the next level. Think beyond your "typical" cash layout for minimum credit card payments or your electric bill. What can you do to make those expenses fit within the available income? Or, can I increase my income to help meet my goals?

Reduce Budgeted Expenses Related to Needs

With your list of "needs" in hand, you can work through some expense reductions. Remember, my definition of needs was limited to housing, food and transportation. Because a whole section of this book is devoted to saving on groceries and food, this chapter will not cover that need.

So, let's first look at your mortgage expense. What is the interest rate you're paying on your mortgage? Can you possibly refinance your loan for a lower interest rate *and* a lower term? We get tempted sometimes by the possibility of lower monthly payments by refinancing a mortgage that we have 20 years left on to a 30-year term. Think about it! You're now adding ten more years of interest to your total due. And, 10 more years of having at least one debt to pay. Moving to a longer-term loan would only be advised if you are just a few years into your current mortgage loan (1-5 years) and you can get a significantly reduced interest rate.

Figuring out if it's worth it involves quite a bit of math, and there are some good resources to help you decide, so that won't be discussed here. Just search online for a mortgage calculator and look for one that has an amortization schedule.

It's almost always better to go to a shorter-term loan (with potentially slightly higher monthly payments) with a reduced interest rate than it is to go to a longer term to lower your monthly payment. If you truly can't afford the mortgage at the current amount, you could try to refinance, or you could sell the home and find a house with a more affordable payment. Yes, it is easier said than done, but it is an option that should be considered if your debt is overwhelming.

If you rent a home or apartment, you might have options to lower your housing payment. First, you could consider moving to a less expensive place. That could mean moving from a larger home to a smaller one, or moving to a less expensive apartment, or even renting a room in someone else's home.

That's a non-starter for some. It might be difficult to find affordable housing in the area you live in, or you're under a lease obligation and need to stick it out at least for the foreseeable future. So, there are other options. If you've been current on your rent to this point, you could try to negotiate a reduced amount - at least for a limited amount of time - with your landlord. You don't have to lay out a sob story. But you need to come prepared with information like your rent payment history - like paying on time and not missing any payments and proof of your steady income. A reasonable apartment manager might consider this, especially if they constantly chase other tenants down for payment.

There is also a possibility to get a discount for paying early, if that's not already part of your lease agreement. If it is, you need to be taking advantage of that. You could also work for the landlord or apartment manager, making minor repairs, doing yardwork, etc. If the landlord can save themselves time or money by having you do this kind of work, it may be worth $100 off your rent.

Utility bills are another "needs" area to reduce expenses. The obvious way would be to reduce the amount of that resource you are using. Natural gas and electric bills tend to fluctuate from month to month, depending on your usage. Turning the thermostat down just a few degrees can have drastic effects on your utility bills in the winter-time – and the reverse in the summer. Reduce the temperature even more at night in colder months. You may get better sleep and you'll save money (resulting in even better sleep!). Consider investing in a programmable thermostat if you don't already have one. While this is an upfront cost, if used correctly, over time it will save significant dollars on your heating and cooling bill.

You could also make a routine to make sure lights and appliances that aren't in use are turned off and unplugged. Why unplug? There is still a trickle of electricity being used even if the device plugged in is turned off.

Other routine maintenance items can help you save a few dollars here and there. Did you know cleaning your refrigerator coils can reduce the energy usage, prolong the life of the appliance, and save money? That's an easy thing to do every 3-6 months and will pay off. Additionally, making sure your furnace filter is changed frequently enough will save money. The furnace becomes inefficient and uses more electricity if the filter is not clean.

Set reminders on your calendar to make sure you're taking care of these routinely. An energy drain that isn't always thought of is leaks around windows and doors. Weather stripping or caulking can help you avoid literally blowing money out the door. There are so many more tips like this. Many states, in conjunction with utility authorities, offer energy audits. The state can suggest a qualified contractor to come to your home and find ways for you to reduce your energy expenditure. Sometimes these are free and sometimes they cost a small fee. In some cases, you can get a reduction on your bills if you follow through with correcting deficiencies found in the audit. And, of course, you'll get additional savings by reducing your energy usage.

Additionally, to help make budgeting easier, you could ask to be put on a budget plan. This may be called by a different name, depending on the area you live in. In general, these plans would make your monthly bill equivalent to the average of your bill over the last 12 months.

Illustration 5

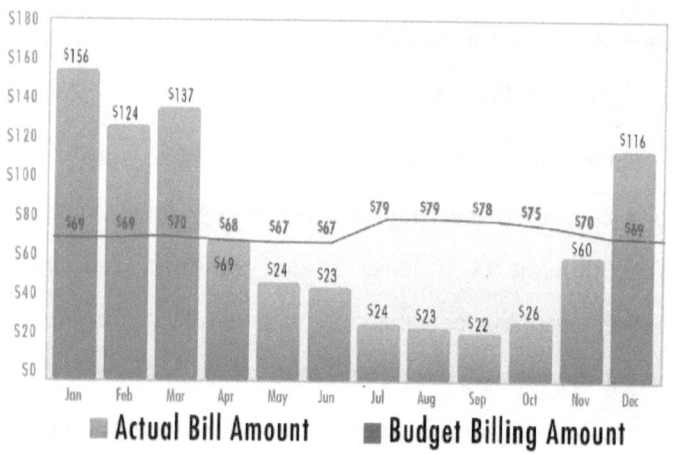

Actual Bill Amount ■ **Budget Billing Amount**

It's much easier to plan for a specific amount in the budget, rather than an expense that may vary by more than $100 a month. Illustration 5 shows an example of the difference between an actual bill and a budget bill. The actual bill varies by as much as $134, whereas the budget varies only by $12. Be aware of your actual usage! Because these plans are almost always based on last year's average usage, depending on how the company figures your payments, you could be left with a hefty balance at the end of the yearly cycle because you used more energy than you did last year.

It might be smart to start in the spring or fall, when heating and cooling are at their lowest use to get a better annualized amount. This could also reduce the likelihood of a large annual adjustment amount. There could be monthly fees associated with doing the budget plan. Be sure to ask questions if it isn't clearly identified in the information on their website or when you're speaking to a company representative.

Now, let's look at transportation costs. Depending on your situation, you might need to get creative to address your transportation needs. Are you making payments on more than one vehicle? How high are the payments and can you really afford them? Would it be possible to go down to only one automobile? Or, you could consider trading in a more expensive vehicle for a lower-cost option. When considering what "more expensive" means, factor in costs of insuring your vehicle and fuel.

For your auto insurance, what deductible and limits do you have? Can you increase your deductible amount to save money? Many people elect to have a lower deductible ($250 or $500), but they could save on their monthly costs if they increased that. By the way, if you do increase your deductible, plan on setting aside part of your savings to cover that increased deductible amount if you ever need it. You might also discuss decreasing your coverage on the vehicle with your agent or splitting your deductible on comprehensive and collision coverage. There are many factors going into that choice, so it's important to understand your state's requirements and how that would affect you. If going down to only one automobile isn't an option, consider consolidating and mapping out routes for errands to save fuel costs. Even if you save yourself $5-10 a month in gas, every little bit counts.

If you are in an urban area with good public transportation, that might be a cost-effective choice. Owning a car in a major city sometimes comes with a hefty price tag - adding expenses for parking garages or parking meters on top of the normal gas and insurance costs. Relying on public transportation could potentially save several hundreds of dollars a month. If you rely on taxis to get around, consider switching to Uber or Lyft - generally these are much less expensive options.

Finally, don't forget the more environmentally conscious, health-enhancing bicycle! Especially for those who live close enough to work and businesses, a bicycle really is a viable option. Even if you need to invest in a bike that is more reliable, or even an ebike, you'll come out ahead financially and physically.

Reduce Budgeted Expenses Related to Wants

This is a broad category, so this section will just cover some of the expenses that the majority will have. These include telephone or cell phones, internet services, and credit cards. You may have included these as needs, and that's ok - the principles still apply.

Do you have a contract with a major carrier for your cell phone? Often, a no-contract phone service is just as good with much lower costs. Unlike some contract carriers that give you the phone for "free" as part of the contract, with most non-contract carriers, you do need to bring your own phone that's compatible with that service, or purchase a phone from them when you start service. Still, in the long run, this saves hundreds of dollars over the contract plans. If you have a contract, you may not be able to get out of it early, but it's definitely something worth looking into.

If you still have a landline in your home, but primarily use a cell phone, you could potentially discontinue the landline service. I've had clients say the "family" needs a telephone number. The truth is that most adults have a personal cell phone and by the time children are getting personal phone calls, they have cell phones, too. (By the way, you could certainly stop paying for the children's cell service. While it is extremely convenient for parents, it isn't a necessity - even if your child thinks it is).

If the kids don't have a phone, you could look at getting another line added to your plan, if you feel that it's important to have a phone designated for the family. Another option is a pay-as-you-go cell phone to use as the home phone, with only voice minutes. When you forgo data and text, the expense is usually much less. Beyond cell phones, one idea that would be worth investigating is magicJack®, Ooma, or similar products. MagicJack® and Ooma use VoIP (voice over internet protocol), so you do need a high-speed internet connection to use the service. You pay for the service either monthly or annually - but the annual price is about the same as one month of a regular landline.

Internet services can be difficult to save money on. Depending on where you live, you may not have many options as far as which provider you use. But you may have a couple alternatives as to the type of service. If you're currently paying for cable internet services, you could check out DSL or satellite. Both have their drawbacks but may be less expensive than cable internet. Another choice is a service called FreedomPop, which is a free internet service – after you pay the one-time fee for their home modem. FreedomPop isn't available in all areas and you do have to pay for increased data beyond 1G per month. If you stream movies, 1G is not enough. Some areas have internet available at a reduced cost for low-income families. The program varies by state and requires proof that you're receiving certain government benefits. If all else fails and you feel like you need some internet service, but don't qualify for the programs, you can always go back to dial-up. You'd have access to surf the web and send email, but you wouldn't have enough bandwidth to watch any videos or play online games.

Cable television is certainly a cost that can be eliminated. So many households stream their television and yet for some reason, they hang on to the cable bill. Just think about it! You can't possibly watch 150 channels of television, or even be interested in half of them! Consider moving to a streaming service like Netflix®, SlingTV®, or HuluPlus®. These are cost effective services that allow you to have a good variety of programming without the huge bill. Of course, there's always over-the-air programming. If you have no money in your budget for cable or even a streaming service, free television is the way to go! I've been doing this for years and don't miss cable at all.

Credit card debt is a big source of stress for many families. The only way you can eliminate credit card debt all at once, without somehow falling into a big sum of money is to file bankruptcy (not recommended unless it is a complete last resort). There are absolutely things you can do to help reduce the amount owed and the interest rate. You won't be adding to this debt because you are following the cash-only plan, right? Even if you will continue to use your card, you should be paying off whatever amount you add to that balance that month plus your budgeted amount to pay off the credit card.

First, let's talk about ways to reduce the debt amount. Aside from getting an unexpected inheritance or bonus, you're probably not going to be able to pay off the debt right away. You can take advantage of the Consumer Credit Counseling Service (CCCS) or credit.org. Credit.org is a non-profit agency that provides debt-counseling along with other financial services to consumers.

There are many CCCS agencies around the country and they may operate a little differently in some ways, but they do all offer the same core services. One of these is the creation of a Debt Management Plan. Usually, part of the plan is consolidating all your unsecured accounts into one monthly payment. They will work with your creditors to potentially reduce the balance or interest rate of your debt. Keep in mind that some debt management plans require you to stop using your credit cards altogether - and at the very least, you are not allowed to apply for new credit. This action will cause your current creditors to reinstate the previous interest rates or reverse any allowances they made for you. Be sure you understand all of the terms and conditions before you enter into any agreement.

If you don't want to enter into a debt management plan, you could negotiate with your credit card companies yourself. You will need to remain calm and pleasant. Remember, you're asking for them to make a special consideration for you and getting upset will not help! It might be useful to have an introductory offer from a competing card to reference. This technique works better if you are a long-time customer with good payment history. Let them know you would like to stay with them, but the offer from the other company is hard to resist. They may be more likely to work with you. If at first you don't succeed, try, try again! Ask to speak to a manager if the person you speak with first can't or won't help. Even if it doesn't work the first time you call, you should continue calling every couple of months. In many cases, persistence pays off.

One special note about credit cards - as you are moving towards living within your means, you could leverage credit cards to improve or maintain your credit score. If managed well, the credit card can be an asset. The FICO score uses your debt to credit ratio - basically, this means how much of your available credit limit you have used - as part of your score.

Keeping your balance at zero, or very close to it, but keeping the account open can be very favorable. For example, if your credit card limit is $7,000, but you have no balance, you have a 0% debt to credit ratio. You have used zero of your credit. But, to keep the account open, you'll need to use the card at least once a year. You could put a date on the calendar to use the card for a small purchase (even something as small as a purchase at a convenience store). Then, pay the balance off by the due date. Some people go as far as literally freezing the card in a block of ice so they aren't tempted to use it often - only bringing it out once a year to use and keep the account open.

Emergency Fund

While paying off debt is important, you need to be sure you have established an emergency savings fund with extra dollars not designated to pay for your needs. Establishing at least a small emergency fund will keep you out of trouble when those unexpected expenses crop up. It may not be completely feasible right away, but your goal would be to save at least enough to cover 3-6 months' worth of the amount needed to cover your needs. So, if your needs budget is $4000 per month, your goal would be to save at least $12,000 that would be easily accessible for living expenses. That number is huge for most people. So, start small. Aim to save one month's worth of expenses and then focus on eliminating your debt so that you can save more. Special note for those that receive SSI (Supplemental Security Insurance - not Social Security Disability Insurance) benefits. Because that program is needs based, you are only eligible if your total assets are below a certain amount. Be aware of what that limit is and stay within the guidelines if you need to continue with the SSI benefit.

Other Factors to Consider in the Budget

I think this is a good time to talk about how to budget your money to eliminate the debt you have. I'll include all debt in this - including automobile loans and your mortgage. After you negotiate the reduced balance or interest rate, you need to think about how you will budget your credit card payments. Make a list of all your debt, including total balance and the interest rate. Determine which debt has the highest interest rate. This is the balance you will pay off first. If you have extra dollars that aren't designated for "needs" you would allocate some of that extra to this debt.

All other debt, you would pay only the minimum balance due every month. You must pay attention to this, though. For credit cards, if the accumulating interest will put you over the credit limit for that card, you may need to pay slightly more than the minimum. Continue with this method until the debt with the highest interest rate is paid off. Then, you will put the entire budget amount you were paying for that debt to the debt with the next highest interest rate. Be aware of any debts, such as auto loans or mortgages that have early pay-off penalties. Even with the penalty, you often will come out ahead because of the money you'll save in interest payments. By the way, for auto loans with an early pay-off penalty, you could check in to refinancing the loan with another bank, which usually eliminates the penalty.

To determine how much extra you'll be putting to debt payment, in your budget you can determine a "lump sum" that will be used to pay all the debt with interest rates. From this lump sum, figure up how much over your minimum payments you actually have to pay extra towards your debt. You can either choose to include your mortgage in this lump, or not. Typically, your mortgage is going to be your last debt paid off. Not only because it's the largest debt, but also because it usually has the lowest interest rate. Once all the other debt is paid off, then all the money that had been going to the other debt will then go to the mortgage.

Consider this example. The budgeter determined that he had $800 a month to put towards his debt. When he totaled all his minimum payments, that came to $763. So, he had $37 extra per month to put towards debt payment. After reviewing his list of accounts, he determined that this extra payment was going to go towards his Visa debt. The interest rate on that card was the same as his Store card. But he'd be paying more in interest every month on that card because the balance was higher. The sooner he could pay that off, the better.

Debt Name	Total Balance	Interest Rate	Minimum Payment	Monthly Payment
Visa	6,000	18	70	107
Store card	1,500	18	25	25
MasterCard	8,000	14.9	75	75
Auto loan	12,350	12	250	250
Discover	3,500	11.49	43	43
Student loan	17,000	5	300	300

Once the Visa is paid off, he will pay the Store card off using the entire payment that was going to the Visa plus the minimum amount that he had been paying on the Store card. That payment would then be $132. Below is the order his debt would be paid and the payment that would be allocated to it because the other debts were already paid off.

Visa $107
Store card $132
Master Card $207
Auto loan $457
Discover $500
Student loan $800

You can see after he paid off the Visa card, the entire $107 went towards the Store card - changing the monthly payment from $25 to $132.

Use the Debt Repayment Plan (Worksheet #4) at the end of the book to get a good visual on your own debt repayment order.

Case Study

Kyle and Becky decided to track actual expenses for about a month before they finalized their budget. That doesn't mean that they didn't work on their finances at all during that month. While they were tracking, Kyle called the electric and gas utilities to find out if they could be put on a budget plan. While they didn't "save" money, Kyle was able to get on a budget plan to make their bills more predictable. Previously, they had estimated the electric bill to be $175, which was based on their highest monthly payment. With the budget plan, their bill would be around $125 per month - their average payment over the last year. Their gas bill would be around $80 a month.

Becky went to work investigating a different cell phone plan. She found a pay-as-you-go option that used the same cell towers as their current plan. The good news was that they were just past the 2-year contract, so they could leave their plan without penalty. The new plan will cost them about $75 a month, with all the same features they had previously. This cut their costs by $125.

The next budget item Becky tackled was their car insurance. She called their current agent, plus obtained quotes from several other insurance companies. She ended up staying with their current insurer, because of their long-term relationship with their agent. But, by simply asking for discounts that might be available, the agent found a couple of discounts they qualified for. Becky also asked for a reduction in their coverage and an increase in their deductible. Their new monthly payment for auto insurance was reduced to $80 - a savings of $45.

Becky and Kyle discussed giving up cable. While it was a big discussion, they decided to give up cable for 2 months, on a trial basis. If they felt like they had to have it back, they would make other concessions to add that back to the budget. They didn't save as much as they thought because their internet service was essential. They did switch internet providers, and their bill every month was going to be about $50. In total, giving up cable and switching providers for internet service saved them $100.

Becky also decided that she could give up her gym membership. This fell into their "wants" list and because she only went occasionally, she knew she could save that $50 for something they really needed. Her hair and manicure appointment was harder to give up, though. She agreed that she could make this appointment every other month, which would cut the monthly expense in half. For clothing and shoes, they opted to change their buying habits (see more in Dressing Well on a Budget). They changed their budget to $50 a month. The other item that came off the wants list was the college savings for their son. This was a difficult decision. Ultimately, they knew they could provide a better future (and example) for him if they could eliminate their debt.

After the month was up, they looked at where some of their more variable expenses ended up. Their gasoline expense was right around what they estimated - it came out to $348. They decided to leave the budgeted amount at $360 in case they had a couple extra errands. They could potentially reduce the cost if they needed to.

Their cash outlay for groceries (excluding dining out) was $700. Additionally, they spent another $215 eating out - sometimes for lunch and sometimes for dinner. This was much more than they expected. Becky decided she could probably save about $20 a month by choosing a different grocery store and using coupons (more about this in Eating Well on a Budget chapter). Kyle agreed to try packing his lunch every day, rather than grabbing fast food. Kyle's lunch expense accounted for about $80 of the dining out expense. While this would add a minimum amount to their grocery bill, it would end up saving about $65 a month. They also agreed that they would only eat dinner out once per month as a family and budgeted $60 for that meal. Because Becky was going to be preparing more meals at home, she decided to change the grocery budget to $725 and they added a subcategory of Dining Out and set that budget to $60.

Once they had established the amounts for their variable expenses, they entered their official budget in the software application they had selected previously. This is what it looked like:

Expense	$ Amount Budgeted
Mortgage	1500
Electric bill	125
Gas bill	80
Cell phone	75
Groceries	725
Dining Out	60
Internet	50
Home insurance	80
Car insurance	80
Gasoline	360
Medical/Dental insurance	600
Clothing/Shoes	50
Soccer League	25
Bowling League	150
Salon	62.50
Total	**$4022.50**

Of course, they still needed to address their emergency savings and their debt payments - 3 credit cards and 2 car payments. Based on their income and the total of their other expenses, Becky and Kyle had approximately $1017.50 to allocate to these payments. Their minimum debt payments add up to $840, so they don't have a ton of wiggle room. Becky decided they should put $125 in an emergency savings account every month. It would take them quite a while to build up the savings fund to what they really need, but at least it was a start. This left them with $52.50 for additional debt payments above the minimum. To decide where to allocate the additional funds, they listed their debts with interest rates and minimum payments.

Debt Name	Total Balance	Interest Rate	Minimum Payment
Car loan 1	$13300	8%	$350
Car loan 2	$8000	10%	$300
Visa card	$8000	18%	$100
Discover	$4000	14%	$60
Target store card	$750	15%	$30

From reviewing the interest rates, they decided the extra money should go to the Visa card because it had the highest interest rate. Becky entered the rest of the budget into the app.

Expense	$ Amount Budgeted
Mortgage	1500
Electric bill	125
Gas bill	80
Cell phone	75
Groceries	725
Dining Out	60
Internet	50
Home insurance	80
Car insurance	80
Gasoline	360
Medical/Dental insurance	600
Clothing/Shoes	50
Soccer League	25
Bowling League	150
Salon	62.50
Car loan 1	350
Car loan 2	300
Visa card	152.50
Discover	60
Target store card	30
Emergency Savings	125
Total Expense	**$5040.00**
Income	
Becky's income	2700
Kyle's income	2340
Total Income	**$5040.00**
Income-Expenses	**$0**

Summary

To create a true budget, you need to look for ways to reduce your monthly expenses related to your needs and reduce or eliminate expenses related to your wants.

- Be sure you have tracked your expenses for at least a month so that you know what your true costs are - tracking for two or three months is better.
- Don't be afraid to cut the cable cord - or eliminate other expenses you had been thinking of as necessary!
- Put extra dollars towards an emergency fund before paying off all your debt.
- Put other dollars towards the debt with the highest interest rate and once that's paid off, move that payment to the next highest interest rate.

You can do this!

Sales, Coupons and Clearance

Introduction

A deal is a deal, right? Well, not so fast... This chapter covers some places to find savings and coupons and how to use them effectively. By effectively, I mean just because an item is on clearance or you have a coupon, doesn't mean you need to purchase it. I'm sure you've heard about people who are "extreme-couponers." They end up getting some items for free, others at a greatly reduced price. You've seen their overstocked pantries or storage areas and you might think you could do that, too. Sure, you probably could. But I'm telling you, it's only partly worth it.

If you are having difficulty making ends meet, there is value in spending time finding coupons and sales and saving as much as you can - that's why I'm writing this chapter. However, you should NOT be buying something simply because it's on sale. Remember the needs vs. wants discussed at the beginning of this book. There are many things we can live without. Most of the things we purchase other than food (and occasionally clothing) should be considered "wants." You need to ask yourself if this is an item your family needs and can use within a reasonable time frame.

I once had a client who was struggling to pay bills and was buried under a mountain of "things." I was helping her organize her home. On one occasion, I discovered that she had just purchased 5 shopping bags of clothing for her children because they were on clearance. I must admit, the prices were fantastic! The clothes were for the baby to wear 6-7 months later. We all know how quickly and unpredictably babies grow. I wouldn't have advised her to purchase the clothes. While finding brand new clothing priced at $2-3 is a steal, not knowing for sure that they could be used and already having too much in the house would put this in the category of wasteful spending.

Coupons

Coupons come in many different forms and for many different things. I'm not just referring to grocery coupons. Those we'll explore in greater detail in the Eating Well on a Budget chapter. Businesses of all types offer a percent off coupon when you enter your email on their website. Signing up can save some money if you don't mind getting a ton of email. Companies use the coupon to get you onto their mailing lists. There isn't anything inherently wrong with this. Sometimes you can even get some fantastic offers. Where I find the email is an issue is when you can't resist every single coupon that comes to you. Some people feel obligated to use it. People feel the time pressure. "Oh no! I only get 30% off tonight!" Then, they spend money thoughtlessly on items they really don't need and aren't in their plan. My advice? Go ahead and sign up for the email list and use the initial coupon if it's a purchase that's in your plan. Once you have what you need, unsubscribe! You can always sign up again when you purchase from that retailer in the future. Besides, think of all the time you'll save not dealing with those emails if you unsubscribe. Time is money, right?

Dedicated coupon sites are another way to save money. If you can imagine it, there's probably a coupon site for it. When researching for this book, I found sites for restaurants, travel, and many other things. Please be very careful when considering using a site. While there are many legitimate websites, there are just as many scams. Some of these are phishing websites. They get you to enter your information to get fake coupons.

You can always check out a website's Better Business Bureau (BBB) rating. Among the legitimate sites, there are some that are better than others - and it depends on what you're looking for. These sites were all operating at the time of this book's publication, and had a decent BBB rating, or weren't listed at all.

RetailMeNot is a great site for a variety of stores. It's not limited to groceries or clothing. The company describes themselves as having "500,000+ coupons for 50,000 stores." The deals are easy to find and use. I have found from time to time that the deal was expired, or it wasn't really a "deal" at all. Sometimes retailers just have their normal sale going on and it's listed on RetailMeNot as a deal. You can choose to sign up for the site or download their app, or you can just browse the coupons and use them. My preference is to just browse the coupons. I did download the app, but the notifications were intrusive.

Another general site similar to RetailMeNot is Offers.com. It has some of the same issues as the other site in that the offer codes don't always work. They also have "deals" that are really just the normal sales offer that you don't need any special code. You can also download their app to get alerts.

DealTaker.com is similar to RetailMeNot and Offers.com in that it isn't dedicated to any particular category, but it is overall different from those two sites. With DealTaker.com, you can browse the coupons separately from the deals, or you can search by store. They also have an entire section devoted to grocery. The coupons listed here come from another coupon site - Coupons.com - which is discussed more in the section about savings on food.

A discussion of coupon sites wouldn't be complete without discussing Groupon. This site (and app) have a bunch of great deals. Use caution with Groupon. It's way too easy to get sucked in to the discounts and you may find yourself surfing through the app and purchasing merchandise, trips and other stuff just because it's too good to pass up. Stay strong! If it's not in the budget and not planned for, don't buy it. Once you gain the financial freedom you're striving for, you'll be able to occasionally indulge in an unplanned bargain. Another note about Groupon is that not all retailers are honest. Please check out the retailer through the Better Business Bureau before purchasing. Some retailers have not honored the Groupon, or only honored part of the offer - making the good deal cost you much more in the end.

Beyond the above-mentioned sites, there are others that are dedicated to specific categories. You can get some great deals from sites like TechBargains which, as the name implies, touts coupons for tech-related purchases, but it does have a huge selection of non-tech deals, as well.

TravelCoupons is another site to consider. Unfortunately, they don't offer deals in every state (and some states have limited offerings). It does offer some good deals if you haven't planned your travel ahead of time, so it's worth checking out. Other sites like Expedia, Travelocity, Kayak, Trivago and Hotels.com are all fine places to check out deals for travel.

If you have a baby or young child, you might want to check out BabyCheapSkate.com. This site has all sorts of deals for just about anything you need for this age group, from diapers to strollers and everything in between.

If you qualify, see if it makes sense to sign up for groups that provide discounts for many products or services. This could include AARP for people nearing retirement age. The membership fee is pretty low ($16 annual renewal) and you can save much more than the $16 by taking advantage of the discounts. AAA is another membership to consider, although the yearly price tag is much higher (around $50). But you don't need to be a senior to qualify. These memberships only make sense if you remember to use the discounts and services they offer. Make it a habit to check available offers before you purchase.

And, then, there are the old-fashioned paper coupons. You may get a weekly free circular that has a collection of coupons for groceries and other items. This is free money if it's something you were going to buy anyway. Take a minute to flip through the pages and clip the coupons you'll use. It only takes 5 minutes - but can save you $15 or $20, depending on the coupons that are available.

You could also purchase an actual newspaper on Sunday. The Sunday newspaper is where you'll find the bulk of your paper coupons, especially for groceries. In general, it's worth the couple of dollars you spend on the paper. Other physical coupons arrive in the mail, usually from stores you've purchased from before, or maybe new establishments trying to obtain business.

Again, consider whether the coupon applies to something that is already within your budget to purchase. You shouldn't hang on to a coupon unless you're going to use it to avoid the pressure of the "buy now" mentality. Think about where you'll stash the coupon, too. For grocery coupons, we'll cover that in the Eating Well on a Budget chapter. For other coupons, you might want to stash them in an envelope in the glove compartment of your car, or if it's for a purchase online, maybe next to your computer or on your desk. The discount does you no good if it's not available when you're spending the money.

Sales and Clearance

Pay attention to sale ads. If you have a bigger purchase on your plan, like furniture, research what you want first. Then wait for a sale to be advertised or for the item to be on clearance. Most of the time, these purchases aren't emergencies, so you can afford to be patient. Research is key. This will keep you from impulse buying, and you will almost guarantee getting a better product at a better price.

Read sites that tell you when categories of goods go on sale. A good place to start is Clark Howard's website, clark.com. Overall, this site is a fantastic resource for anyone looking to save money or avoid getting ripped off. Just type "best time to buy" in the search box and you'll get multiple articles on when to buy things like cars, houses, appliances and more. Consumer Reports also has great information on when to get the best deals. They created a month-by-month listing of when to find the best prices on products. The bonus with Consumer Reports is that you also get the product ratings. Depending on what you're looking for, you do need to pay a membership fee to get the full list of product ratings. If you are on a really tight budget, this is an expense you can do without.

Using clearance sales can be a great way to buy the things you need. Again, it's important that you aren't buying just because it's a good deal. First, be sure you need the clearance item. If it's not on your plan or an immediate need, walk away. Even if it's something you may need in the future, be aware that buying too far ahead of when you can use it may cost you in the long run. For example, clothing you buy ahead may no longer fit, or circumstances might change, and you no longer need the item you purchased. Be thoughtful about what you buy and why you are buying it!

If you're shopping online, you could save quite a bit by using rebate sites. Rakuten is a very popular site that gives you cash back on your purchases if you start your shopping from their site. Basically, they get a commission for sending customers to the other stores. Rakuten "shares" the commission with you. I found cash back offers from 2% all the way to 10%. So, there could be significant money back, depending on what you're buying. Add the Rakuten internet browser extension and you will get a notification any time there is a rebate available from that site you're shopping on. I routinely get quarterly rebate checks totaling $20 or more simply from using Rakuten when purchasing items I was purchasing anyway.

As a side note, before you purchase on any site, you could also use other browser plugins to track prices and make sure you're getting a good deal. Check out Honey (joinhoney.com) or Camel Camel Camel (camelcamelcamel.com). These are two of the more popular plug-ins, but there are others worth checking out.

Store Discount Cards

Several retailers offer store discount cards that provide special discounts or cash back on purchases. The "cards" come in several varieties. Quite a few are simply loyalty cards. The card gets scanned when you make your purchase (or you enter your card number when purchasing online), and you receive a sale price or discount on some of the items purchased.

Other cards actually function like credit or debit cards. I don't typically advocate for using debit cards for any reason, as there are fewer protections under the law. But if you can receive a percentage of your purchase as cash back or a discounted purchase price for using the store card, it might be worth the risk. An example might be a store discount debit card for gasoline purchases that gives you 5 or even 10 cents off each gallon of gas. That could result in significant savings.

Price Comparison

What if you forget your coupons or come across something that seems like an amazing deal? There's an app for that! In fact, several apps. I'm referring to price comparison apps that you can download to your smartphone. In general, you just scan the QR code or barcode of the product you want to check prices on. The app will return a list of other places you can get the item and for what price.

Some apps compare the price and offer coupons. Two worth mentioning here are ShopSavvy and The Amazon App. ShopSavvy, in particular, is highly rated. This app returns both online and local deals when you scan a product. It lets you setup price alerts for products you're shopping - finding both online and local deals. They also have a few "best time to buy" reports on popular items like televisions and computers.

Additionally, check out BuyVia, which is a free app for both IOS and Android. It's similar to ShopSavvy and will show you coupons offered for specific products you're shopping for.

Outside of barcode scanner apps, there are a multitude of other price comparison websites that specialize in comparing prices on things like flights and hotels, and gasoline. I've listed a few in the Resources chapter. One to note for every-day use is Gasbuddy.com. Because fueling a vehicle is a "need" if you must own one, it makes sense to routinely search for the best prices on gasoline.

Summary

When using coupons, don't feel pressured to use every single discount that comes your way. It's not a deal if you don't need it. Take advantage of coupon sites and apps. See a complete listing of all the referenced websites in the Resources listing at the end of this book. Double-check the website's Better Business Bureau rating before using to avoid scams and rip-offs. If you're using physical coupons, put them where you're most likely to use them.

Plan your major purchases so you have time to research them. That way you know a good deal when you see it. Use price comparison apps to find the best deal. Wait for a sale or clearance to save more money and only buy if it's in your budget plan.

Jennifer Raschig

Eating Well on a Budget

Introduction

You have to eat, right? You might as well find ways to reduce this necessary expense. The goal is not to make you eat rice and beans for months on end (although, those are tasty from time to time). You can learn to look for bargains, use coupons effectively and find alternative places to shop. Doing this will help you save money without having to eat the same foods over and over again. When we're focused on getting to financial freedom, dining out should be a rare treat. To save money when eating out, look for deals using ideas from the previous chapter. This chapter is devoted to saving money specifically on groceries.

Planning

One of the biggest helps to saving money on groceries is having a plan for what to buy. This can be done several ways. A great way is to plan your meals for the week, make a list of groceries needed for those meals, add staples that you are out of, and voila, a plan for what to buy! Yes, making a meal plan can be time consuming and you have much better things to do. Think of it this way - spending an hour making a meal plan and grocery list will help you avoid making multiple trips to the store. This results in spending more than you need to on gas and food because you didn't plan for those purchases.

Of course, there are meal planning apps that can be useful. It might take some experimenting, but you may find one that's helpful to you. Many of the meal-planning apps have recipes incorporated into them, and I won't get into the pros and cons of those apps in this book. However, they are certainly worth researching and using if you won't make a list without one. If you decide to use an app, be sure you look for a free app or find a free trial before spending money. Rather than getting an app, try using a spreadsheet to house your meal plans and grocery list (see Illustration 6). Simple, but effective, and best of all - free!

Illustration 6

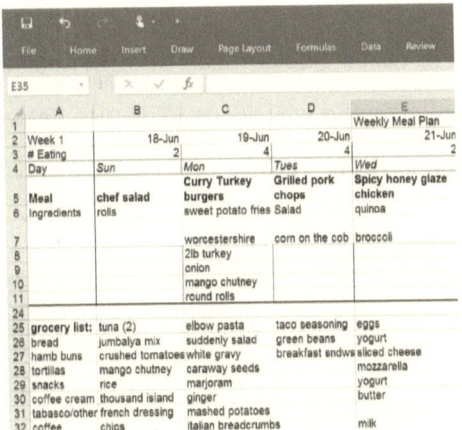

	A	B	C	D	E
1					Weekly Meal Plan
2	Week 1		18-Jun	19-Jun	20-Jun	21-Jun
3	# Eating		2	4	4	2
4	Day	Sun	Mon	Tues	Wed
5	Meal	chef salad	Curry Turkey burgers	Grilled pork chops	Spicy honey glaze chicken
6	Ingredients	rolls	sweet potato fries	Salad	quinoa
7			worcestershire	corn on the cob	broccoli
8			2lb turkey		
9			onion		
10			mango chutney		
11			round rolls		
24					
25	grocery list:	tuna (2)	elbow pasta	taco seasoning	eggs
26	bread	jumbalya mix	suddenly salad	green beans	yogurt
27	hamb buns	crushed tomatoes	white gravy	breakfast sndws	sliced cheese
28	tortillas	mango chutney	caraway seeds		mozzarella
29	snacks	rice	marjoram		yogurt
30	coffee cream	thousand island	ginger		butter
31	tabasco/other	french dressing	mashed potatoes		
32	coffee	chips	italian breadcrumbs		milk

Use the weekly sales ads to create your meal plan. This is more cost-effective than just randomly coming up with meal ideas. For example, if you can get ground chuck for $1.98 per pound versus $3.00 per pound, this week, plan to make a meal or two with that. Yes, this takes a bit longer than just having a rotation of meals, but it makes a difference in how much you need to budget for food - thus leaving more for the not-as-necessary things. Also, plan to buy seasonal produce. Often, this is less expensive than out-of-season fruits and vegetables - and it tastes better, too. One of the best places to get in-season produce is by checking out a local farmer's market. Check out localfarmers.org to find one near you.

Scouring the sale ads is time-consuming. But in this modern era, you have some short-cuts available to you. There is a website called 5dollarmealplan.com that sends you a weekly meal plan and grocery list. You also get access to some coupons and deals. Each of the recipes are created to cost less than $2-3 per person. This does cost $5 per month but could be worth it if you have difficulty planning your own budget friendly meals, especially when you factor in the coupons.

Grocery Coupons

If you get free coupons in a weekly advertiser, by all means, clip those if they are for groceries you are already buying. You could also purchase a newspaper that has coupons. Be sure if you're spending the money that you take the time to clip the coupons. Otherwise, physical newspapers aren't worth the price.

In the previous chapter, you learned about several coupon websites and apps. Grocery coupon apps were specifically left out to be discussed in this section. Again, be sure to check out any website or app with the Better Business Bureau before using, as their rating may have changed since this book's publishing. Someone could probably write an entire book on the available grocery coupon websites and apps, so this book will just include sites that have been around for a while or have amazing deals.

SmartSource is one of those that's been around for quite some time. You might recognize the name if you browse the paper coupons in your Sunday paper or weekly circular. Often, those coupons are SmartSource coupons. You can tailor the search to your local area and clip a few coupons without creating an account, which is nice. However, you'll be shown more coupons if you create an account and log in. ValPak is another name you might recognize. Like SmartSource, they have physical coupons in newspapers and other weekly circulars. Valpak's selection of coupons is better than SmartSource. Both sites are easy to clip coupons and print them.

Coupons.com is probably the most well-known grocery coupon website - and it also has a mobile app. Most of these websites are similar in features and coupon content. You search for the coupons you'll use, "clip" them and then either print, or download to a store savings card.

Ibotta.com (with available app for mobile) is a bit different from the other sites I mentioned. The basic premise is that you buy specific products from stores in their network and you get "cash back" once you submit proof of the purchase. Sometimes the product is brand specific and sometimes it is generic. So, for example, you might be able to buy any brand of milk and get cash back just for buying milk from that store. Savings can really add up when you combine Ibotta with other coupons. Incidentally, Ibotta also offers coupons and discounts for much more than just groceries - both in-store and online - with additional savings if you "pay" with Ibotta at select stores.

A word of warning though - Ibotta does collect information and wants to know your location. They use the location to offer appropriate rebates, but I realize some people are uncomfortable with giving up this bit of privacy. As with all the coupon and rebate sites, only buy what you need. Just because they offer a rebate doesn't mean you need to buy.

Price-matching

You can also reduce your grocery expenses by shopping at stores that have price match guarantees. Typically, with these guarantees, there's a lot of fine print you need to watch out for. Most often, competitor's pricing that includes a "bundled" price or limited quantities won't be price matched. Getting through all the details can be tedious, but you can use the policy to cut down on your time in shopping by not having to go to multiple stores and save money at the same time. Often, it is up to you to bring in the ad from the competitor that shows the lower price. If that's the case, be kind to your fellow shoppers. Have the item in the competitor's ad circled and write the price from the store next to it. The cashier can then find the item more quickly to enter the difference. An even bigger time-saver (and dollar saver) is to use the store's app to do it for you. Check to see if the store you shop at has an app with this feature. Depending on what brands you buy these savings can add up quickly.

Store brands and package sizes

One of the best ways to save money is to buy the store brand. Many people think that the store brand is usually an inferior product. Research has shown that the store brand is often the same as the national brand. The packaging is just different. You've been taught not to judge a book by its cover, right? Same principle goes for store brand food. Even with using a coupon for a national brand, the store brand is often less expensive.

Be aware of unit pricing with both national and store brands. Package sizes are often the same, but they hold different product volumes. It's important that you know how to calculate the per unit price to make sure you're getting the best deal. Some stores list the cost per unit on the product's price tag on the shelf. Look there before you spend time calculating. If you do need to figure the unit cost yourself, all you need is a simple calculator. Divide the total price by the number of units. Units can be individual items in a package (for example a 12-pack of soda), or ounces, etc.

Don't be fooled by sale prices. Always check the per unit price. Also, bigger is not always better - although bulk prices often are. Just do the math (I know, it's probably not your favorite thing), and you'll always get the best deal.

Alternative stores

You don't always need to shop at a traditional grocery store. In fact, you typically get better deals shopping at warehouse clubs or discount supermarkets. Shoppers can save anywhere between 20 and 30% off regular grocery store prices at these locations. That can equate to a couple thousand dollars a year!

When considering shopping at a warehouse club, like Sam's Club® or Costco Wholesale®, consider how much you'll save and determine if the membership fee is worth it. Most often it is, but you should take advantage of a "free day" at the club to compare per unit prices on items you buy most often. If you can see that the savings on a few items would more than pay for the membership fee, then go for it.

Make sure you have a plan in place to not over buy. I cannot stress this enough! If you don't have a plan when you walk in, you will be tempted by all the options (the giant container of cheese puffs!) that are available. You'll spend money on things you don't really need just because you've never seen a 5-gallon jar of pickles before. If it's not on the list, don't get it. If it's in a container that's too big for you to use up in a reasonable amount of time, don't buy it. You need to be able to use up what you buy before the expiration date. Your family may not appreciate eating a perishable item (think fruits and vegetables) multiple times a day! If you can't use what you buy, you're wasting money.

You also need to have adequate storage for your purchases. Maybe consider sharing a membership and purchases with a friend or family member. Then you can cut the cost of the annual fee while avoiding the inherent storage problems with bulk buying. Although this chapter is focused on groceries, if you are considering a warehouse club membership, be certain to take advantage of all the membership has to offer. Usually, there are other necessities that can be purchased at a much lower price - like gasoline - that could make the membership an even better decision.

Discount supermarkets are another option that can help you save on groceries. I'm not talking about Walmart (although, in general, Walmart is less expensive than traditional supermarkets). I'm referring to stores like Aldi, Family Dollar, Dollar General and new-comer, Lidl, with a few locations. With each of these stores, there are pros and cons. If you really insist on purchasing name brand foods, then you'll most likely not want to shop at these locations. If you can get past that, though, you can save real money.

Aldi has very small stores and generally has only the Aldi's store brand available. They do carry national brand products as well, but not many - and it varies from day to day what might be available. The store brand items are generally comparable to national brands, but at a much lower price. You bring your own bags and pack your own groceries to save the store overhead costs, which they pass on to you. A bonus with shopping at Aldi is that you won't have to deal with making decisions. There is only one option for most products, so it takes much less time to shop. Aldi is a personal favorite of mine.

You can also find deals at Dollar General. Be aware of the per unit price here, as well as at Family Dollar. What might seem like a bargain may not be. Other discount stores may be available to you, depending on where you live. The stores I mentioned are not limited to one specific region of the country.

One more type of store to consider is a salvage or "scratch and dent" store. Salvage stores carry items that may be dented, or just past their "sell by" date. While most stores consider these unsaleable, they can be a great option for those looking for a deal. Most packaged food can be used after the sell-by date, so don't let that deter you from shopping here. To find one near you, just do an internet search for salvage grocery stores or scratch and dent groceries.

Summary

Reducing food expense is important to staying on track for your budget. An absolute necessity is creating a plan. Whether you choose to do this with an app or on paper, be sure you have a grocery list before you go shopping to cut out impulse buying. Take time to plan your menu around store sales ads so you can maximize your budget. Shop at stores that price-match to save you time and money. Clip coupons like crazy! Compare prices by figuring out the unit price of an item so you know what the best deal is. Finally, consider alternatives to your local supermarket. It's possible to save up to 30% or more by shopping at warehouse clubs, discount supermarkets and salvage stores.

Dressing well on a budget

Introduction

Clothing is not on my list of necessities - yet we do need to be clothed (at least in most communities). While clothing shouldn't be a regular purchase, you do need to plan for this expense and know where to look to find deals and save money.

Resale and Consignment Shops

If you've had experience with poorly organized or maintained resale or thrift stores, you might be cringing at my suggestion to shop at one. But you can save significant dollars on clothing that is in great condition. If you look hard enough, you can even find designer brands. Many resale shops are charitable organizations, so you can score a great bargain and help someone in need at the same time.

There are some money-saving tips to keep in mind when going to a thrift shop. First, as with so many things I recommend, go in with a plan. If you're shopping for jeans for your daughter, don't start in the women's dress section.

Go in with a set amount to spend - and armed with knowledge of what a good deal looks like. Even in resale shops, some prices are too high for the item. On a recent trip, a pair of jeans was almost $10. That may not sound like a lot of money, and the jeans were in great shape. Considering, however, these were not brand-new jeans, and my budget was less than $10, I did not buy them.

Often, these stores have sale days, making a deal go from good to great. If you know when the sales are, you can save your clothes shopping for the sale days. Before you purchase anything, though, try it on. Returns may not be allowed. If it doesn't fit, you're wasting money if you can't return it. Even if you can return it, you'd be wasting time doing something you could have avoided. While you're trying the clothes on, check for ripped seams, broken zippers and other repairs needed. If you can't fix it, don't buy it. Most of the time it's not worth the money it would cost to have someone else make the repairs.

Location of the resale shop can also make a difference. Shops in wealthier neighborhoods tend to have higher quality clothing, probably because the residents of the neighborhood are bringing their items to their local thrift store. You also might have a larger selection in these neighborhoods because they tend to not have as many customers as shops in less-well-off communities.

Shopping at consignment shops is similar to most other resale shops. You also have the opportunity to sell your own clothing (usually name-brand clothing, in good condition) at many consignment stores. Some may even take your clothing in trade. This is a great option if you have children who grow out of their clothing rapidly and it's still in great condition.

Incidentally, although this chapter is focused on clothing, resale shops are fantastic resources for other household items you may need. Again, be prepared with a list and stick to it. When you've budgeted well and climbed out of debt, you can use thrift stores even more for those items on your wants list.

Clearance Shopping

I'm sure you might be able to guess what I'm going to say about clearance... that's right - have a specific list of what you're looking for before you begin your trip. I know I seem like a spoilsport. We're talking about your financial freedom here. There will be a day when you can spend the extra $5 on that impulse buy - but today, that $5 could be put towards paying off your credit card debt or building up your emergency fund. Keep that in your mind when you're shopping - it makes your choices a little clearer. Here's a tip - take a picture of the item. Wait 72 hours. Then, revisit it to see if you still feel like you need it. Usually giving yourself time and space away from making the purchase will help you gain clarity on the purchasing decision.

Check out clark.com and consumer reports to find the best time to purchase clothing. Also, stores often have seasonal clearance items available long before the season is actually over. Check out the clearance racks (almost always located at the back of the store) a couple months before the season has "ended" to start getting good deals. Another trick is to shop on a Thursday. Because stores frequently are busier on the weekends, they begin putting new items out on Thursday to prepare. The older items are marked down and moved out of the prime spot. Shopping on Thursday lets you avoid the crowds, take advantage of good deals and have a better selection of merchandise because it's not already picked over.

Have patience when you spot an item that you need and it's not yet on clearance! By taking notice of the shop's sales cycle, you can likely time your purchase to score a better price. Many stores leave new merchandise out for 6-8 weeks before marking it down. Where you shop may be different, so don't assume. But you can start watching for patterns and snag the item when it's at its lowest price and before its gone. Practicing this is another strategy to avoid impulse buys.

Online Consignment Stores

Online consignment stores are a somewhat newer option for the bargain hunter. Each of them operates slightly differently. The basic premise is really no different than physical consignment shops, except it's on a much larger scale. While prices are generally good, some of the sites also offer percent-off discount codes occasionally that make this an even better buy.

Perhaps the most well-known online consignment shop is ThredUp, which features clothing for women and children. In general, ThredUp has very high-quality standards for items it accepts, so it's certainly a step above the traditional thrift store. According to their website, they only accept about 40% of the items that are sent in. The site is laid out very nicely and makes it easy to find clothing and shoes in your size. They often have coupons available for even better deals. The nice thing is, if it doesn't fit or you determine after you receive it that the damage is unacceptable, you can return the item for store credit. You would be wise to "save up" a list of items to buy from the site as free shipping doesn't kick in until you've spent $79 (at the time of this writing).

You can also potentially make a little money from ThredUp, too. This is where the consignment part comes in. You can order a bag from them so that you can send in your clothes for resale. Once your item is accepted, you set an initial price which will be open for bids. After the bidding window, the item can remain on the site for 60-90 days, depending on the brand. Once your item has sold, you get paid. They either pay you through Stripe, PayPal, or store credit with one of their partner shops. You can also choose for them to donate your earnings to a charity in your area. The charity is limited to a few, but you do have some choices. If they don't accept your item, you can choose to have them return it to you. That comes at a price, though. Additionally, items not returned to you get sold to third-party sellers or textile companies.

Poshmark is another site that might be worth browsing. Unlike ThredUp, there isn't a "store" that processes the clothing and ensures that the quality is good, although they will authenticate items that are listed as a luxe brand. You'll find more than women's clothing here. They also sell clothing for everyone and housewares. Basically, other people list their for-sale clothing and accessories on the site and you can purchase from them. Sometimes, the seller might be willing to do a bundle deal or take another item in exchange. You can score some great finds here, and if the clothing isn't what you expected, you can get a refund through the site. Of course, you can also sell your own clothing here to make some extra cash. For most listings, they take 20% of the sale price and you keep the rest. They also handle the shipping to the customer and all customer service issues.

One other online consignment worth mentioning is Swap. Swap is newer than some of the other sites listed, but still has been around a few years and has seen tremendous growth. The online store started as a children's clothing consignment and has expanded to include adult clothing. They are very restrictive in what they accept, so the clothing seems to be in excellent condition. They do have a clearance section on their site as well, although the criteria for clearance isn't clear. The deals seem to be slightly better than what's listed on their other pages. You do need a minimum of $60 for free shipping, so buy for the entire family at once. You can also return the item if it is damaged or otherwise misrepresented. Selling on this site is a bit more difficult. You must be invited to be a premier seller. Your payout depends on what they price the item at. You get either 15% or 70% - $4.95 fee.

Exchange Parties

Exchange parties, also referred to as swap parties, are relatively unheard of in some circles, but worth exploring. You just need some friends or family willing to exchange clothing with you. The premise is that everyone brings items in good shape that they (or someone else in their family) just doesn't wear anymore. These can be fun ways to get new things for free and get rid of clothing you no longer want or that no longer fits. When putting together the guest list, keep in mind the approximate sizes of the guests so that everyone has a selection. If exchanging clothing for children, or other members, be sure to invite guests with children of same gender and similar size.

Keep in mind that you should set some rules for the party. Be sure it's clear how many items each person should bring (or have a minimum number of items with no upper limit). Set up a way for everyone to look at the clothing before any swaps are made. It's probably a good idea to only allow each person to take home the same number of pieces that they brought. If it's not fair, it's unlikely your guests will be game for parties in the future. There are many ideas on Pinterest for how to host a successful swap party.

Walmart and other discount retailers

I left this one for last because people have very strong opinions about Walmart. Whatever your opinion, if you're looking for decent new clothing at a reasonable price, you can't beat the discount retailers. And, the deals are even better when clothing is on clearance. I have found brand new clothing for less than resale shop prices here. I know the quality isn't always the best, but when you're shopping on a tight budget, you can't always shoot for the highest quality. Other stores, like Dollar General, and Family Dollar, have reasonable prices, as well. Dollar General, for example, has regular clearance sales and available coupons that could save you quite a bit of money. The selection isn't always great, though. Just keep an open mind and be selective about your purchases. If you believe that brand name clothing is synonymous with higher quality, you might consider Ross Dress for Less. They routinely offer 20-60% off retail prices. You won't get Walmart prices, but you can be assured of getting better-than-retail deals. Ross only has physical locations, no online shopping, which helps them keep their prices lower.

Summary

You have a lot of options for dressing well without spending a lot of money. Remember, you should only buy what is necessary and have a budgeted amount to spend on clothing. Only buy what you can afford. Check out thrift shops and learn when they have sale days to get the best deals.

Don't be shy about buying clothing at discount stores or on clearance. You can often get new items for less than you can get used clothes if you keep an open mind. Consider buying clothes listed on online consignment websites. These sites usually have great offers and it's much easier to browse online than in a thrift store. And, for the least expensive (free!) option, host an exchange party with friends to swap out clothing you're no longer interested in for something new-to-you.

Entertainment - Free and Cheap

Introduction

Life on a budget doesn't have to be boring. You just need to find new ways to be entertained. If you have been going out every weekend to a bar or maybe have date nights at high-end restaurants, my suggestions might not be what you had in mind for entertainment. Broaden your horizons, keep an open mind - and be prepared to be entertained.

Going Out

We all need to get out of the house and do something different on occasion. You might be surprised at all the local fun there is to be had. One of the best ways to find out what's going on in your community is to contact your chamber of commerce (online or in-person). The chamber usually has lists of events that are going on in the community along with the contact information of the event host so you can find out more. Most community offerings are either free or very low cost. These events range from art walks to outdoor concerts to farmer's markets and everything in between. If you do go to an event like a craft fair, you don't need to buy to have a good time. You can get ideas for things you may want to do, catch up with friends or meet new people in your town - all without spending a dime.

Checking out local museums and zoos for their event schedule is also a great way to save some money. Most have a free day or reduced admission days. One zoo in my area has regularly scheduled free days on weekends through the slower winter months. This is a great alternative when you're tired of sledding and skiing! Mark these days on your calendar so you don't miss them. The only downside to the free admission days is that the venue can be somewhat crowded, because everyone else wants to take advantage of the deal. Don't let that stop you! You can still see quite a bit, and you can always return to see what you missed the first time around.

Consider being a tourist in your home town. See the streets and shops through fresh eyes. Take a camera along to capture the sights. You might be amazed at what you find if you just walk around for a few hours. Some cities have sculptures placed in various locations you can make a point of admiring. You can scope out old or modern architecture. Stop and smell the roses at a local florist shop. Take pictures everywhere! You never know, you could turn out to be a fantastic photographer and sell those prints!

Part of being a tourist in your community is enjoying biking and hiking trails that might be a little out of your way normally. There are usually trails for everyone, from more strenuous treks to paved paths. Visit a state park to take advantage of all its natural resources. This isn't always a free option (depending on the state). If you don't know where your state parks are, search for them online. Also, visit the National Park Service website - www.nps.gov - to find nationally designated parks near you. Visiting these parks can be great half day or full day trips. Pack a lunch and head out. Make it fun for small kids by creating a scavenger hunt. Or, better yet, stop at the ranger station where they typically have nature programs for kids - for free! For even closer to home fun, have a picnic at a local park. This would be good for a couple of hours of entertainment if there is playground equipment, tennis or basketball courts, or green space for yard games.

Another cool thing to do with the family is geocaching. Geocaching, in case you don't know, is like treasure hunting with a GPS device. Although it peaked in popularity a few years ago, there are still tons of geocaches out there, with new ones being added quite frequently. You can look up caches in your local area at the Geocaching.com website to find the coordinates and then set off on your way. Geocaching is also a fun thing to do when you're on vacation or in a different city with a few hours to spare. Some require hopping in the car to get from location to location, other trails are hiking trails with various caches hidden along the way. Finding the cache is not always easy. The GPS coordinates only get you so far, then you have to search. Some are out in the open, but more often than not, the cache is cleverly hidden. What's in it when you find it? Well, that depends. Sometimes, there's a logbook to sign, or just a message to read. In other caches, there are things to see or take a picture of. Or, you can leave something of your own. You never know what you'll find and that's a big part of the fun.

If you haven't considered it before, volunteering is a great way to get out and about. Find out what organizations in the community need your help. Get the entire family involved. Habitat for Humanity is one option, but there are so many more. Try out volunteermatch.org to find a cause that your family can participate in. Usually, it only costs you time. The rewards are so much greater.

Staying in

If spending time away from home isn't your thing, there's lots to do at home (or in someone else's home) besides watching television. You could host a game night with friends, or even just have a weekly game night with members of your household. This is a really great way to stay connected and have a good time. Set some ground rules - like turn off your cell phone and everyone participates - so that it truly is a time to bond. Have a variety of games available. If you don't have any games, you can almost always find them at rummage sales or resale shops for much less than the original cost. You can play so many games with just a deck of cards, too, so don't think you need to have a fancy "board" game. When having friends over, have everyone contribute to the snacks so one person isn't spending too much. Alternate houses to change the scenery and share the hosting responsibilities.

You could also join or start a club - whether it's a book club, photography club or cooking club, there are always others around with the same interest. MeetUp is a great online resource to use for just about any type of club or group. This website is sectioned into categories of interests so that you can "meet up" with other like-minded individuals. You can go into any of the interest categories, click on a group and get basic info about the group. Then, request to be added. Some of the groups have specific requirements for membership, but many are open and welcoming. When I did a search in my local area, I found kayaking clubs, photography groups, Mensa groups and even a book club. Facebook is another place to find groups or clubs. Just click on "groups" and either select a category or group displayed, or type what you are looking for in the search bar and see what comes up.

If you're interested in book clubs in particular, there are other resources to help you find an existing one. Your local library is a good (and logical) place to start. Many libraries have several book clubs based on book genre. Ask about posting an announcement there if you are starting your own club. GoodReads, another online resource, also has book clubs to join.

You could combine the game night idea with the club and join or create a gaming club. Check online for Dungeons and Dragons® or Magic® clubs, or other board game clubs. I found several gaming groups in MeetUp with a variety of games played. There truly is something available for every type of gamer.

Another "staying in" idea is to host a cooking night with friends. Each person brings ingredients for recipes. You hang out for several hours together making food and enjoying the fruits of your labor. This gives you all a chance to try some new foods without spending too much on going out to eat. The bonus is the time with your friends. Often, the cooking night has a theme and the menu is planned. You could even decorate in that theme (as long as you aren't purchasing items) if you really want to make the night special. The point is to have a good time without spending a lot of money.

If you want to be more active, but don't want to go out, have a family dance party. Designate a family member to be the DJ and select the music. Come up with creative dance moves. Have a competition to see who has the best rhythm. The best thing is no one outside your home can see what a terrible dancer you are! This is even fun to do with friends. You save some money by not going to a club, but still get to do what you love. If you miss the live band, throw in some karaoke. Ok, I know that's not for everyone. But it can be a blast. You can find free karaoke songs by searching the web or download a free app to your phone that has some great music. No need for a microphone, just get up and belt it out.

Summary

Don't let living on a tight budget keep you from having fun. So many opportunities to get out and spend time with neighbors, friends and family are available. Just be willing to keep an open mind and try new things. Check out your chamber of commerce or Facebook for local events or join a new club on MeetUp. Spend more time with your family indoors or out. It's not how much you spend when you're together, it truly is the experience that will be remembered.

If ends just don't meet - or you want to get ahead faster

Introduction

What happens if you track your income and expenses, reduce every way possible and you still don't have enough? Then, find ways to earn additional income. You're probably thinking easier said than done. I know, for some, just getting one job is difficult, let alone adding a second. There are many options these days, especially for those who are comfortable working virtually.

Virtually endless possibilities

If you have time to work, but possibly can't get to a job, or maybe need to be home to take care of children, you should consider some of the many online opportunities. There are sites dedicated to connecting those who need work done to those who are available and have the skills needed. On Fiverr.com, you can get paid $5-$10 to do small tasks. True - that's not a lot of money, but if you do 10 tasks at $10 each, you have an extra $100 for the month - no small change!

VirtualAssistants.com is a longer-term income generator. In essence, this is a job board with only virtual jobs. The difference is that the jobs are pre-screened so that potential scams are weeded out. There is a fee to become a member, though, so be sure this is the route you want to take before registering. Alternatively, you can use Upwork.com. This is for all sorts of skills. You add a profile with an hourly rate. Those who may need your services invite you to interview or contact you to do work for them. Payment is made through PayPal. This is a fantastic way to earn some money on the side.

You could also consider secret shopping. This is a great opportunity to earn up to a couple hundred dollars a month, depending on how much time you can put into it. Basically, companies pay you to purchase items or interact with store employees and then write a detailed review on the "shop." Be very careful, as there are many scams with secret shopping. You should never pay a fee up front to become a secret shopper. Follow the tips for protecting yourself on MSPA-NA.org, a trade association focused on customer experience.

Sell Something

You don't necessarily need to be skilled to sell stuff online. What you sell is completely up to you, but there is a knack to it if you want to generate serious money. I'm sure you've heard of and maybe have even used eBay. That's not the only place to sell your goods, but it's an easy place to start. Be sure you know the value of what you're selling. Start with things you already own so you aren't investing money up front. Then, use the money generated from your first few sales to find things at garage sales, thrift stores, or on clearance to resell at a higher price. Do some research to know what others would be interested in. You can't pick up a bunch of low-quality clothing and expect to make any money. Find things that you know a lot about and can recognize high quality or rare items.

If you're creative, you can sell things you make. Etsy is an online store that sells unique handmade items from artists all over the world. The possibilities are endless! Don't limit yourself to physical goods. Photographers can also generate a small income online by selling high-quality digital images to Shutterstock and other online stock photo distributors. Keep in mind, this is not for the amateur photographer. There are strict image quality requirements that must be met. You do need to know how to manipulate images in photo-editing software and understand lighting, among other things, to be really successful.

For electronics, use a site like Swappa.com or other resale sites. Be sure to follow the guidelines for posting your item and shipping with tracking information. This will help to protect against any potentially fraudulent activity or scammers.

Drive to success

Maybe you've used Uber or Lyft to get around at some point. Did you ever consider driving for them? Picking up a few fares a week can generate that little bit of extra cash you need to pay down your debt. Or, if you don't want to drive other people around, maybe you can consider delivering packages or other items. People post "gigs" for drivers to pick up. The concept is to pick up a gig for a location you're already traveling to or going near so you're not really going out of your way. You save the other person time and the cost of shipping and packaging and you get paid for very little work. Now you can even drive for Amazon - check out flex.amazon.com.

Start a side business

Figure out what skills you have to offer and start your own business. It doesn't have to be a crazy big idea - maybe you are really good at fixing things. Put a post on Facebook Marketplace letting people know what you can do. If your rates are reasonable and you can provide some references, chances are, people will give you the opportunity. Of course, having your own business can get more complicated at tax time. You may want to consult with a tax professional and/or do a lot of research before you go this route to avoid any issues. Remember though, your business can be just about anything you want it to be and often you can get started with very little or no money invested in it.

Summary

I realize that not everyone can cover their current expenses. If you've cut your spending, looked for ways to save and still can't get ahead, looking for new ways to make money might be the best solution. You don't have to get a second job at a brick and mortar location. Consider selling things online or using your skills and experience to generate an income from home. Even if you are able to cover your current expenses, looking to generate a little more cash every month will enable you to get out of debt sooner and experiencing the financial freedom you've been waiting for!

Getting Ahead and Staying Ahead

Introduction

Congratulations! You've made it through a lot of the tough stuff. Well, at least you now have the tools to make it through figuring out how much money you really need to live on. You have taken steps to reduce expenses and establish a true budget. You may be a few years away from getting out of debt, or just a few months. Either way, you are ready to think about getting ahead and staying ahead. You see, all the previous chapters in this book were just helping you to "get back to zero." To really be free financially, you need to take steps to save money for your future.

The tips in this chapter should give you some hope that there is life after debt, and you can have true financial freedom. To get ahead financially, you need to consider how to take care of unexpected expenses or loss of income, create savings for fun things, and how to plan for retirement.

Emergency Savings Fund

If you recall, I recommend a little bit of an emergency fund before you start paying off debt. Hopefully, you've taken steps to establish this as part of your monthly budget. At this point, you should have at least a month's worth of living expenses saved up. This is the minimum amount that may be needed if you were off work for a couple of weeks due to illness or injury, or if you need to cover an unexpected expense like car repairs. You shouldn't stop there.

There needs to be enough to cover a longer term, too. Just think, if you were finally getting caught up on your debt, but then you couldn't work, or you were laid off. You'd just spiral back into living week to week and have to start over (although with a different mindset than before). To avoid that, it's best to have 4-6 months of necessary living expenses saved in an emergency fund.

The emergency fund needs to be easily accessible. You shouldn't invest this money in stocks or tie it up in certificates of deposit (CDs). You won't be able to get to this quickly. Find a savings account that yields interest to stash your money until it's needed. An excellent place to look is on

BankRate. You can look up savings or money market accounts by how much money you have to invest. Some banks require a minimum deposit amount, which is fine. Find a bank or local credit union that has a decent interest rate with no monthly fees and no penalties for going under a minimum balance, in case you need to tap into the fund.

Once you establish the amount that you can contribute routinely, try to have that portion of your paycheck automatically deposited into your savings account. Don't use this account as "fun" money. This should be strictly used for unexpected expenses, or to pay for budgeted necessary monthly expenses if you no longer have an income. If you want to establish savings for vacations or gifts as part of your budget (which I highly recommend), these should be in their own accounts so you can easily see what you have available for each category.

Just like with the credit card debt, once you have an adequate emergency fund you can divert the money that was going into the emergency fund into another "getting ahead" idea.

Retirement Savings

If you're just beginning this journey, you may think you can never retire. However, if you keep on with your plan to live within your means, retirement will be in your future. You have several options for how you save. Which options you choose will be dependent on your individual situation. At this point, I will give the standard disclaimer that you may need to consult with a financial advisor and/or a tax professional to determine which option might be best for you.

Although there are varying opinions, usually, investing routinely over time is the best way to go, rather than thinking about it once per year and throwing a lump sum in. This is called dollar cost averaging. Dollar cost averaging has a couple of advantages. One, you can plan for the investment amount and add it to your budget every month. You can almost "set it and forget it." Two, your investments generally will cost less over time because you buy fewer shares when the price of the investment is high and more shares when it is low. Plus, you don't have to worry about 'timing the market' (figuring out when investments have bottomed out or gone up as high as they're going to before you buy and sell).

Living Below Your Means

For example, if you consistently invest $200 per month over the course of 5 months in a mutual fund, the number of shares you buy each time will vary based on the current market price of that fund. The price may go up or down, but, over time, you'll be paying an average of all those prices. While you may not get the lowest price, you also won't be paying the highest price for the majority of your shares, either. In the example below, using dollar cost averaging, the investor spent $1000 and paid an average of $12.40, giving him 82.47 shares. If he had waited until month 5 and dumped in $1000 to buy the mutual fund, he would only have 66.67 shares because the share price was $15. His $1000 does not go as far. His investment market value would have been $1000, rather than $1237.

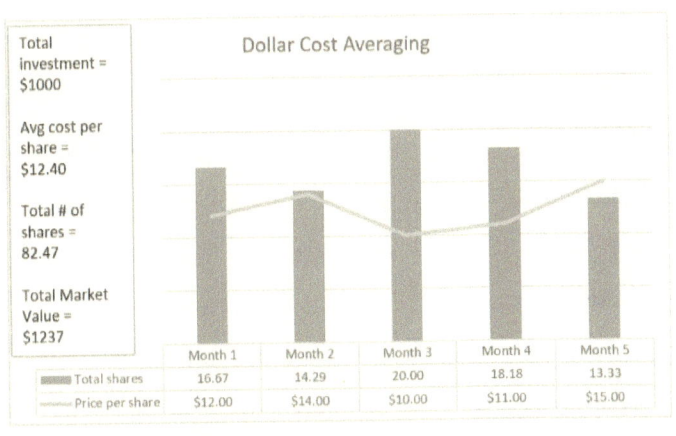

	Month 1	Month 2	Month 3	Month 4	Month 5
Total shares	16.67	14.29	20.00	18.18	13.33
Price per share	$12.00	$14.00	$10.00	$11.00	$15.00

Total investment = $1000

Avg cost per share = $12.40

Total # of shares = 82.47

Total Market Value = $1237

Dollar Cost Averaging

Could he have a higher market value if he had dumped in $1000 in month 3 when the price was at its lowest? Well, yes, but it is impossible to time the market to know you are investing at the lowest price. The price could go up or down at any time - it is unpredictable. Using dollar cost averaging allows investors to have a safer investment strategy to get a more favorable average price. And, if I lost you with that explanation, just remember - add to your savings in smaller amounts monthly rather than one big amount once per year. Now, having said that, I'll cover investment options that may be available to you to for retirement planning.

Does your employer offer a retirement plan? Many employers do. There are basically seven different types of investment vehicles that are offered by employers. While pensions were very popular in the past, if your employer now offers one, consider yourself lucky. In the United States, pensions are typically fully funded by employers. The employee doesn't have any control over how the money is invested. When the employee retires, they get a set monthly amount which is usually determined by the employer based on how long the employee has worked for them and the employee's income. While pensions are nice, many companies are doing away with them. Also, unlike 30 years ago, many people do not work at the same employer for their entire lives. So, it's good practice not to rely entirely on that income for your retirement. There are no guarantees.

Currently, 401(k) plans are the most common retirement plan offered by organizations. With a 401(k) plan, you designate to invest a percentage of your income into the plan. There is a limit to how much you can invest annually - and when you reach age 50, you can contribute a little more to "catch up." Some companies even offer to match your contributions up to a certain percentage. At a minimum, you should contribute the amount needed to get that match. That's free money! For example, your employer has a 401(k) plan and offers a dollar-for-dollar match up to a 4% contribution. Basically, this means you get an additional 4% in pay that goes directly to your retirement. Who wouldn't take that deal? 401(k) contributions are tax-free. This means that whatever income you contribute to the plan, you do not pay income tax on that amount in the year that you contribute it to the plan. If you can, bump your contributions up so that you are saving the maximum allowed. The allowed amount generally goes up every year, so you'll want to review and adjust accordingly.

The earnings from your investment are tax deferred. So, you don't pay income tax on any of the money until you withdraw it from your plan in retirement. An early withdrawal penalty of 10% of the amount withdrawn applies if you take money out of the plan before a set age. The rules on this get a bit complicated. Just know that, especially before age 59 1/2, you will most likely be penalized if you take money out of the 401(k). Also, with these plans, you are required to take a minimum distribution from your plan beginning at age 70 1/2. Again, there are exceptions. That's why it is important to engage the services of a tax professional or financial advisor, if you are unsure of the rules yourself. Profit sharing plans are similar to 401(k) plans in many ways, except generally, the company also contributes a portion of their profits, rather than matching a percentage of your pay. The amount of the employer's contribution will vary, of course, depending on how profitable they were. Sometimes you may get the maximum percentage defined in the plan and sometimes you'll get nothing.

Another type of employer sponsored retirement plan is a 403(b) plan. A 403(b) is the tax-exempt organization's equivalent of the 401(k) in for-profit companies. These plans are funded by the employee and sometimes, the company contributes a matching percentage. So, if you have this type of plan, as with the 401(k), you'll want to contribute at least the amount to get the maximum matching.

Similarly, 457 plans are used for state and local government employers and a Thrift Saving Plan (TSP) is for federal employers. The unique aspect of 457 plans is that if the employer offers both a 457 and a 401(k), you can contribute the maximum amount to both plans. I know that seems like an impossibility right now, if you're just seeing the light at the end of the tunnel. It's important to know, though, so if you ever are in the situation to save more for your retirement, you know you can save double what others can. Also, these are considered "non-qualified" retirement plans, which means there is no penalty for early withdrawal of the funds - unlike 401(k) and 403(b) plans.

Self-employed? You have the option of using an SEP (Simplified Employee Pension). SEPs are based on Individual Retirement Accounts (IRA). An IRA is not associated with any employer. Instead, it is an option to save for retirement on your own. Qualifying to open an IRA is based on income limits. Also, you may be eligible for a tax deduction, depending on your adjusted gross income. Again, see your tax professional to understand if the IRA is a good choice for you.

Usually, the amount you can contribute to an IRA is less than the amount you can contribute to your employer's 401(k). You may be able to contribute to both. There are many banks and investment companies that offer IRAs. It's important to find one that has low fees. Otherwise, you're giving up hard earned money paying for the administration of your account. You don't pay taxes on your earnings in the account until you withdraw the money in retirement. Penalties exist for early withdrawal of the money - 10% before age 59 1/2. Exceptions do exist. If this isn't an SEP-IRA, you can contribute to an employer plan, like a 401(k) and an IRA. This gives you the opportunity to potentially have even more tax savings. You do need to check with your tax professional to determine the best choices for your specific situation.

An alternative is a Roth IRA. A Roth is different from a Traditional IRA in that the you get no tax deduction on the contribution amount. However, all your earnings are tax-free. This means when you withdraw your money, you pay no taxes at all. Incidentally, there are sometimes Roth 401(k) or Roth 403(b) plans. These are great options for many people. A very general way of determining if this might be a good option for you is to consider if you will be in a higher tax bracket when you retire. If so, a Roth plan could save you a lot of tax dollars (and remember, the earnings are tax free, too). Obviously, that is a broad generalization and each situation is unique. Consult a financial advisor to determine what is the best option.

A SIMPLE is another plan that is based on IRAs. SIMPLE stands for Savings Incentive Match Plan for Employees. Smaller employers, with fewer than 100 employees, that do not offer 401(k)s or pensions sometimes use the SIMPLE-IRA as an alternative. There is a maximum contribution amount for SIMPLEs that is more than a regular IRA. The employer also must contribute either a 3% matching amount for employees that contribute to the plan or a mandatory 2% for all employees.

Beyond the seven most common retirement savings offered by employers, you can choose to invest on your own for your retirement. I've already talked about IRAs and Roth IRAs, and if you can invest in those plans, you should. You could also invest outside of actual retirement accounts, although you won't enjoy any tax benefits, either with the initial contribution or with the earnings and withdrawals. I'm referring to typical non-retirement investment accounts with a traditional or online brokerage where you can invest your after-tax dollars.

What should you invest in once you start contributing to one of these plans? I find people are hesitant to invest because they don't understand the different types of investments and what each means for their money. This, however, is not a book on investing or investment types, so I won't go into a lot of detail. I will, however, give a brief summary of the four most common types of investments - stocks, bonds, mutual funds and exchange-traded funds (ETF).

When you buy stocks, you are purchasing a small part of an individual company. You are a shareholder and get to vote on certain things. There is more than one kind of stock, but most often, you will purchase common stock. Your investments in stock can grow through dividend payments and/or growth of the value of the stock (you get these gains when you sell the stock for more than you paid for it). Stocks are considered a risky investment, but also have a high reward potential.

Bonds are basically loans to a company - and just like when the bank makes you a loan, you get back the money you 'loaned' plus some interest. Generally, bonds are considered less risky than stocks. There is some risk, however, because there's a chance the company will not be able to pay back the bond.

A mutual fund is an investment vehicle that is actively managed by a professional. When you purchase a share of a mutual fund (not a share of an individual company), you're pooling your money with other investors. The fund manager takes that money and uses it to buy stocks, bonds or other investment types depending on the type of mutual fund. These funds charge an annual fee and sometimes a commission. The funds aren't traded in the market exchanges like stocks, but you can buy shares through brokerages.

The fourth type of common investment is an exchange traded fund (ETF). ETFs are similar to mutual funds in that you are investing in multiple securities at once through a fund. However, ETFs are different in a few important ways. ETFs usually are investments that mimic a particular market index, like the S&P 500. They most often are passively managed, and therefore have lower fees. And, they can be bought and sold like stocks. The easiest "set-it-and-forget-it," usually low-cost way to invest your money is an investment in an ETF that tracks either the total stock market or the S&P 500 indices.

Your available funds, comfort level and knowledge of investing will influence which of these options you might consider. Nothing is guaranteed and there is a level of risk associated with all these options. But, if you have maxed out what you can contribute to a retirement account and still have cash leftover, you would do well to consider investing more, especially if you want to have money accessible before age 59 1/2.

College Savings

College savings for your children should be absolutely last on your list of things to save for. You should have adequate retirement savings (or at least you are routinely saving for it and the funds will be sufficient to carry you through retirement). Really, if what you are currently saving for retirement will not be enough, then do not even consider college savings for your children. That might seem unfair and you may feel obligated to help them pay for school. But children have so many funding resources for college. You do not have any other sources to fund your retirement. You can't get a loan, grant, or scholarship to support you through your golden years. Besides, when your children actively contribute to funding their own education, it is much more meaningful to them. Trust me, I know from experience.

If you are in a position to save for your child's college education, you have a couple of options that could have some tax benefits for you. Remember that tax law does change from year to year, so consult irs.gov or your tax professional to make sure this advice is still current.

Many people have heard of a 529 plan, but a less popular option exists - the Coverdell Education Savings Account. Each plan has pros and cons. The 529 plan earnings are not subject to federal taxes, and in many cases, are not subject to state tax, with the stipulation that the earnings are used for expenses related to college education. The Coverdell is similar, except the earnings are subject to state tax.

You might consider the Coverdell if you are sending your children to a private school because the Coverdell earnings can be used to pay for K-12 education expenses, as well as higher education. A 529 plan can only be used to cover college tuition and related expenses. There is a contribution limit of $2000 for any beneficiary for the Coverdell per year and the 529 does not have a limit.

Another difference between the two is the age limit for the beneficiary. A 529 plan does not have an age limit. If your children decide not to go to school, you could switch the beneficiary over to yourself or another relative (visit irs.gov to see which family members can be beneficiaries), and as long as the money is used for college, you will not pay a penalty. The beneficiary of the Coverdell must be under age 18. So, with all the limits to the Coverdell, why would you want to invest in this account type? Well, unlike the 529 plan, you can choose your investments. You aren't limited to the options available in the specific 529 plan you have invested in.

	Coverdell ESA	529 Plan
Contribution Limit	Yes	No or very high limits
Contribution tax free	No	Maybe (depends on Adjusted Gross Income
Tax deduction on earnings	Yes, Federal	Yes, Federal and (some) State
Age limit	Yes	No
Income limit	Yes	No
Can be used for K-12	Yes	No
Free choice for investments	Yes	No- limited to options in the 529 plan of the state you select

529 plans are often a better option. You aren't limited to your state's plan, either. You can investigate different state plans to see which have lower administrative costs and better investment options. Clark.com has a guide to 529 plans that is very helpful - the leg work is done for you. Keep in mind that if you invest in a plan other than your own state's plan, you probably won't get the state tax benefits of contributing to the plan, if any were available. In 2019, only 7 states gave a deduction for contributing to a 529 plan from any state.

As with your other investments, contribute routinely to reap the benefits of dollar cost averaging. Another thing to consider is that when your child is applying for financial aid, if they are listed as the beneficiary, this money will count as their money and may lower the amount of financial aid they receive. You can avoid this in a 529 plan by listing yourself as the beneficiary until your child needs access to that money. Of course, from then on, when they reapply for aid, it will be considered in the calculations.

Case Study

When we last visited Kyle and Becky, they had just established their true budget and had committed to cutting other expenses so they could get out of debt and live the life of financial freedom they were longing for. If we fast forward a couple of years, we'll see that they were able to get their debt under control by staying focused on their goal and resisting the pressure to spend money on unnecessary things. While some expenses went up, like insurance, they were able to adjust their budget to accommodate the increase. Now, they are ready to turn their attention to the future.

Becky determined that they would need to save just over $20,000 to have approximately 4 months' worth of income. All the money that had previously gone to paying their debt was now available to either roll into their emergency savings fund, or pay down their mortgage, which they didn't include in their original debt repayment plan. After paying off all credit cards and car payments, they had just over $800 a month to use! They decided to put an extra $500 a month towards their mortgage to get that paid off sooner so they truly would be out of debt.

At the same time, Becky looked into investing in the 401(k) retirement plan offered through her employer. She found out they would match a contribution of up to 6% of her income. Free money! 6% of her before-tax income is about $218. She set that up immediately. You'll see in the monthly budget, that her income is "reduced" but that money is being taken out of her check before it's deposited in her bank account. The $218 is being automatically contributed every month to the 401(k). This money is taken out before taxes, so the amount shown in the budget is approximately how much her take home pay is reduced by the 6% contribution (approximately $134). The rest of the money gained from paying off debt would be put to the emergency savings fund. Once the fund was built up to $20,000, they would move that money to the mortgage.

Expense	$ Amount Budgeted
Mortgage	2000
Electric bill	125
Gas bill	80
Cell phone	75
Groceries	725
Dining Out	60
Internet	50
Home insurance	80
Car insurance	80
Gasoline	360
Medical/Dental insurance	600
Clothing/Shoes	50
Soccer League	25
Bowling League	150
Salon	62.50
Emergency Savings	383.50
Total Expense	**$4906.00**
Income	
Becky's income	2700
401(k) contribution	-134
Kyle's income	2340
Total Income	**$4906.00**
Income-Expenses	**$0**

Kyle and Becky still had a plan for every single dollar. While it was tough for them to stick with the budget, they will be enjoying the benefits of their discipline for years into the future.

Summary

Your head might be spinning after reading this chapter, so hopefully this summary will help to clear it up for you. It's very important to get ahead in the right order. You need to plan for emergencies so that you can continue to stay ahead before planning for other future items.

1. Save 4-6 months' worth of living expenses in an easily accessible savings account.

2. Invest in your employer sponsored retirement plan using dollar cost averaging. This means putting a set amount in routinely versus a lump sum once per year. Contribute at least enough to get the matching contribution from your employer, if they offer that.

3. The type of plan that is best for you will depend on your unique situation. Consult a financial advisor or tax professional for help. You can find a fee-only financial advisor in your local area at www.napfa.org. Be sure to ask them if they act as a fiduciary in all aspects of their business.

4. Don't rely solely on social security benefits or a pension for your retirement. These may not be around by the time you retire.

5. Let your children worry about their college tuition. It's good for them! If you feel like you must contribute, look into a 529 plan that has low fees and potential tax advantages, but only after you have started saving for your own retirement.

The Next Level

Introduction

What if I told you that you could choose to stop working earlier than the "normal" retirement age with just a little more effort and focus? No, I'm not talking about those people who make six figure salaries. I'm talking about people like Becky and Kyle, people like you and me that make very average (and sometimes, even below average) incomes.

This is true financial freedom. Once you achieve this next level, you can be free to choose how you spend your time. You can continue working if you want, you can spend more time with your family, or you can choose to focus on a passion project. That's the beauty of financial freedom. The secret is saving a higher percentage of income than you do currently so that eventually, you have enough to retire on. I'll get to how much that needs to be in a bit.

So, what percentage of your income should you save? It depends. It depends on how much you earn and how much you spend. You have a bit of an advantage over others, though, because you've just learned how to save money on all sorts of things to get your necessary spending down to a minimum. Once you pay off all your debt and establish your emergency fund, you can continue to live below your current income levels and save all of that money!

Savings as a Percentage of Income Explained

First, let's figure out your current savings rate. You need to know two things - your current income and how much you live on. You have access to most of this information in your worksheets, so it should be relatively easy to figure out your savings rate.

You will add up your savings in all accounts (your 401k or other retirement account and any bank accounts or brokerage accounts). Next, divide that total savings by your total take home pay (figure your take home pay by subtracting all taxes from your gross income shown on your pay statement). You want to include any amount automatically saved in retirement accounts, because technically, you do "take that home," it's just moved automatically from one place to another. After that, you'll convert the result to a percentage. Don't worry, if you are math impaired, I'll walk through this with real numbers next.

Living Below Your Means

In our example with Kyle and Becky, their savings rate is currently at 11.4%. Not too bad (more than most Americans), but it won't get them financially independent before normal retirement age. Here's how I figured their savings rate. Let's start with Becky's take home pay. Her pay statement shows that her gross income for the pay period was $3,633. The taxes taken out of her pay amounted to $715. So, her take home pay was $3,633 - $715, which came to $2,918. Becky gets paid monthly. Be sure that when you are looking at your pay statement and figuring your savings rate that you are using the same time period for all your numbers.

Kyle's gross income on his pay statement is $1,200 and his total taxes are $120. Because Kyle gets paid every two weeks, we'll have to do a few more calculations to get his monthly income. We can't simply take his pay statement and multiple that by two because that would leave out two paychecks per year. So, we'll need to first figure his annual income, then his monthly income.

To compute Kyle's annual income, we'll take his pay statement gross amount and multiply that by 26. If he gets paid every two weeks, he'll get 26 paychecks per year (52 weeks in a year divided by two). For Kyle, that will come to

$31,200 before taxes. His yearly taxes taken out of his paycheck will be approximately $3,120. At this point, we can subtract the taxes from the income, giving Kyle an annual income of $28,080. Finally, to figure his monthly take home pay, we take that annual income and divide by twelve. In this case, $2,340.

Now, we'll add up Kyle and Becky's take home pay - $2,918 + $2,340 = $5,258. They don't currently have any income from other sources besides their main job, so we're done figuring monthly take home pay.

Let's move on to their savings. Right now, they are saving $383.50 towards their emergency savings and Becky is contributing $218 per month to her employer's retirement plan. That comes to a total of $601.50 per month in savings.

The last step is to divide the monthly savings by the monthly income. $601.50 divided by $5,258 is .114. This converts to 11.4%. I know that seems very long and involved, but it is relatively easy. I've included the steps for you below.

Here's the formula in steps:

1. *Figure your take home pay.*

Gross Income - Taxes = Take Home Pay

2. *Convert your take home pay to a monthly amount if you get paid weekly or bi-weekly*:

Weekly:

   a. Gross Income x 52 = annual gross pay.

   b. Total taxes x 52 = annual total taxes taken out.

   c. Annual gross pay - annual total taxes = Annual take home pay.

   d. Annual take home pay / 12 = Monthly take home pay.

Bi-weekly:

   a. Gross Income x 26 = annual gross pay.

   b. Total taxes x 26 = annual total taxes taken out.

   c. Annual gross pay - annual total taxes = Annual take home pay.

   d. Annual take home pay / 12 = Monthly take home pay.

3. *Add up all sources of monthly income.*

4. *Add up all amounts you are putting into savings of any kind, including amounts automatically deposited from your paycheck into your employer's retirement plan.*

5. *Convert the savings to a monthly number if needed.*

6. *Calculate your monthly savings rate.*

Monthly savings / Monthly take home pay = Monthly savings rate.

Saving at a low rate like 11% is not going to allow you to be financially independent earlier than the norm (unless, of course, you make an astronomical income). Every little bit counts so don't be discouraged. What needs to happen now is to focus on increasing that savings rate. You can do this by either cutting more expenses or by increasing your income.

Next Level Expense Cutting and Income Increasing

There are several chapters of this book focused on cutting your expenses. If you've taken every single tip, you're probably at the next level already... but, most people only do the minimum they need to in order to get their debt paid off.

So now, I'm asking you to take another look at what you decided to cut back on and what you didn't. First, focus on some of your major expenses - housing, transportation and food. Are you still living in a large, single-family home? Can you sell that house and move to a smaller home? Give it some thought. Many people immediately answer no. They feel like there are too many barriers to selling a home and moving. However, this one move can potentially save you $1000 a month.

If you are a single person, or a young married couple without children, can you share an apartment, or even just rent a room in someone else's home? Often, you can get your housing down to a few hundred dollars a month this way.

Even better, consider buying a duplex or other multi-family building. Live in one of the units and rent out the others. If you can afford the down payment (and there are ways to make this happen), then this is a great way to live for free or almost free. Your tenants will pay your mortgage. A great resource to learn more about how to do this the right way is www.biggerpockets.com/guides. You'll find a guide titled "How to Buy a Duplex: The Ultimate Step by Step Guide" that will help you immensely if you choose to go this route.

To cut transportation costs, you probably didn't consider giving up your car before. But, if you're saving for financial independence, it might be worth riding a bike around town or taking public transportation, rather than paying for insurance, gas, parking and maintenance on a vehicle. Another consideration might be to go down to one vehicle - or trade in your gas hog SUV for a more economical (and overall cheaper to insure and maintain) car.

In the chapter Eating Well on a Budget, you learned how to create meal plans based on sale ads and to use alternate grocery stores and coupons to save money. You can make a game out of this by trying to spend no more than two dollars per person per meal. I know that doesn't sound like much, but it's absolutely achievable using the ideas in that chapter. Based on that, for a family of three, the food budget could be $558 a month. That can be rounded to an even $600.

In my own life, I budget $600 a month for groceries for a family of four. Yes, I shop at Aldi and Walmart and I use coupons and create a meal plan based on sales ads. I would budget more, but two of the family are only here half the time, so I count them as only one person for the budget.

Finally, overall to cut expenses, consider geoarbitrage. What is geoarbitrage? It's making a conscious decision to relocate to an area that has a lower cost of living so that your money goes further. For example, if you live in San

Francisco, California, you will need a higher income to live. Housing and food are much more expensive than many locations, especially those in the southern part of our country.

You could even consider an international move. While it's not for everyone, cost of living in countries like Portugal, Thailand or Costa Rica are much lower than in the United States. If you're interested in checking out other countries, www.nomadlist.com/fire has a calculator for cost of living and how that would help you on your path to financial independence in specific cities and countries.

After those larger expenses, look at the rest of your budget to see if there is something you're willing to cut out to achieve financial freedom even earlier. For Kyle, he might consider exchanging his bowling hobby for something that costs less. Becky might decide that she doesn't need to pay for someone else to highlight her hair. The point is not to deprive yourself of things you truly enjoy. Financial freedom is not about deprivation at all. It's about learning what matters to you most and working towards that.

Next, even if you were able to cover your debt with your current income, it may not be enough to get to a higher level of savings. Now is the time to consider if you need to start a second job or your own business outside of your regular employment (also known, for some reason, as a side hustle).

Re-read the chapter If Ends Just Don't Meet - Or You Want to Get Ahead Faster. Create a list of three to five ideas that are feasible for you to do. Then, pick one and get started.

If that's too scary for you, you have a couple of other options. The first one is also intimidating for many people - ask for a raise. Nothing ventured, nothing gained, right? There is no law that says you can't ask for more money if you are a good, valued employee who does excellent work. It helps, though, to go about it in a thoughtful way.

First, time the ask right. If your company typically gives pay increases at a certain time (maybe around the end of the year, or possible your anniversary date), then be prepared to have a discussion with your boss just before that point. If you've had a pay increase within the last year, it's unlikely that you'll receive another unless your responsibilities have changed significantly, so be sure you account for that. Also, set up time to discuss your salary specifically so that you're not catching your boss at a bad time, or when he or she is rushed.

Second, know what you should ask for. Don't go to the meeting with a wildly out-of-whack request. If you currently make $18 an hour and you ask for a $10 an hour raise, you'll probably be laughed at. Instead, do your research on what is the typical range for someone in your position and with your experience. You can use a website like www.salary.com or www.payscale.com to determine this. You can also ask trusted coworkers or others in the industry about typical pay ranges. It would be better to phrase it in a way that doesn't directly ask them what they make, such as "What would you expect this type of job to pay at a company like I work for."

Lastly, be prepared to talk about why you've earned a raise - and don't focus on the fact that you need or want the money. Emphasize what you've accomplished since your last raise and highlight any new responsibilities you've taken on. You don't usually need to do a formal presentation, but it might be helpful to have a document with these things noted. If your boss has to take the request to someone else to get approval, having a document prepared will help them make your case.

A final way to increase your income is to find a different job altogether. I realize it's not always easy to land another job that pays more, but it's definitely worth exploring. This is especially true if you've not looked for a while. You never know what opportunities are out there for you.

25 Times Your Annual Expenses

How do you know when you've saved enough to have gained financial independence? The conventional wisdom in the financial independence community is that you've reached your goal when you've saved 25 times your annual expenses (or more accurately, 25 times your annual *spending*). The premise is that you can withdraw 4% of your savings portfolio every year (and increase that amount as the cost of living increases according to the consumer price index) and have your nest egg last for at least 30 years. This is based on a study called "The Trinity Study," a report written in 1998 by three professors at Trinity University.

To put this in real numbers, our example couple, Kyle and Becky, would need to save $1,471,800 to retire "early." This number is their $4,906 monthly expense times 12 to find their yearly expense ($58,872). Then multiply $58,872 x 25 to get their savings goal for retirement. This does not take into account any other income they might have after they stop working, like social security - which wouldn't factor in until after normal retirement age.

While I believe that's a good rule of thumb, it won't necessarily work for everyone. There are a number of factors that go into how much you should save in order to have enough to last through your retirement. Some of that is dependent on you and some is dependent on how the markets perform over the years of your retirement.

A better rule might be to save 30 times your annual spending. Saving this amount will provide cushion if the markets underperform or you have a bit of lifestyle creep. Lifestyle creep can sometimes happen if you've achieved financial freedom and you're not being as careful with your money as you were when you were paying off your debt and starting to save for the future. If you want to learn *a lot* more about how much to save and, once you achieve financial independence, how much you can safely withdraw, check out earlyretirementnow.com and the safe withdrawal series on that site.

Saving over a million dollars might be daunting at first, but it's absolutely achievable. Remember, it's all about the mindset and focus. Figure out what you value and work towards that. If it's more important for you to have a lot of things now and work for the rest of your life, that's fine. That's your choice. But if you want to live a life of abundance (abundant time, abundant choice), focus on reducing the acquisition of things and saving for that abundance in the future.

Bonus - Travel Hacking

Introduction

Now, do you want to take your new mindset to the next level? Even if you haven't quite achieved the financial freedom you're looking for, there are ways you can still have a nice vacation and not break the bank. I'm talking about travel hacking.

This is not for the person who still has trouble paying off their credit card balances every month. So, if you struggle with that, set this aside until you have more organization and control around paying your bills. Travel hacking requires a certain amount of discipline in paying off your credit cards (because you don't want to end up in the debt you were in to begin with).

This is not for someone who still has a not-so-good credit score. In order to travel hack, you need to be eligible to open credit cards. With a poor credit score, you won't be able to do that. If you still have a score below 670, it's unlikely that you'll be approved. It's even better to have a credit score above 740. If you don't know what your credit score is, you can get it for free from Credit Karma.

I also want to point out that this is NOT a comprehensive travel rewards guide. The programs change too often to make that good content for a book. My goal is to introduce you to the idea so that you know what's possible and where to start.

The basics of travel hacking

The very basic premise of travel hacking is using travel rewards from credit cards to travel for free or very little money. I'm not just talking about airline miles, either. You can also book hotels and sometimes rental cars with your rewards points.

You sign up for specific cards that give you these rewards and then you use transfer partners to fly where you want to fly. Often, these cards have sign-up bonuses that give you a huge amount of points if you spend a specific amount in a certain time period. The best way to meet that spending goal is to use the card for all of your normal expenses, rather than using any other credit or debit card. Of course, you shouldn't be spending more money than you normally would just to get the rewards.

No, this isn't a scam or illegal. Credit cards want you to sign up and try to earn points because the majority of people put balances on their cards and then don't pay them off. The credit cards can collect interest. You, though, will not let that happen. You'll pay off your balances every month, so you win with travel rewards, but the credit cards don't get any more of your money.

Choosing the right cards

To figure out which credit cards you should open, you need to have a good idea of the type of travel you'll be doing, domestic or international, and how many people will be routinely travelling with you.

Next, use Google Flights (www.google.com/flights) to see which airlines fly to the destinations you'd like to visit. Then, determine if those airlines belong to an "alliance." These alliances are important when figuring out where your points can be used.

After you've determined those things, you can start looking at which card programs will get you the rewards points for the destinations, airlines or alliances you want. While the rewards programs change somewhat frequently, there are a few credit cards that typically offer great rewards and travel partners.

Some cards are more often recommended than others because of your ability to get sign-up bonuses and point transfer options. Chase Ultimate Rewards are probably the most flexible. There are several cards in the Chase program that you can use for this. Some have annual fees, and some don't. You'll need to use your judgement in figuring out if those fees will be worth opening the card to get the travel rewards.

The other card program that is usually important to consider, especially for domestic travel, is Southwest Airlines branded card. With this card, you can potentially earn a companion pass, which allows a companion to fly free with you for a year. As you can imagine, this will add up to a lot of money saved, if you travel frequently.

Using your points

This is where it gets complicated. It can take time to research where you can transfer your points to get the best value. Only transfer points out of your credit card program when you're ready to make the transaction. Often, you can't transfer them back (and so they lose their flexibility) if you don't use them.

Because transferring points can get complicated, it's important that you have the most up-to-date information. My advice is to use a guide to walk you through all the possibilities. The best guide I have found is www.travel.choosefi.com. You can sign up for their free course on travel rewards. You'll be sent an email every day with the lesson (or you can binge on the lessons all at once, if you're impatient). They even give you access to a spreadsheet that helps you keep track of your cards and rewards programs.

While travel hacking isn't for everyone, it can be a smart way to make your hard-earned-dollars go further. Be sure to know the time frame that you need to meet the spending target in so that you get the bonus. And, no matter what, pay off your balances every month to avoid interest charges and fees.

Monthly Needs and Wants List - Worksheet 1

Worksheet #1

Needs	$ Amount	Wants	$ Amount
Total Needs		Total Wants	

Money Coming In - Worksheet 2

Worksheet #2

Source	$ Amount
Total Income	
Subtract $ amount of Total Needs (from Worksheet 1)	
Total Extra $ or Gap	

Budget Planned Vs Actual - Worksheet 3

Worksheet #3

Planned Budget for: _____ (month)		
CATEGORY: _____		
Expense name	Budget $	Actual $

Debt Repayment Plan - Worksheet 4

Worksheet #4

Debt list

Debt Name	Total Balance	Interest Rate	Minimum Payment

Debt Repayment Priority

(In general, pay higher interest debt first)

Debt Name	Total Balance	Interest Rate	Minimum Payment	Monthly Payment

Jennifer Raschig

Resources

Introduction

I wanted to give you one place to find all the software, apps, coupons and other resources I've referenced throughout the book. You can also access the worksheets online at www.jenniferraschig.com/books.

Planning Tools Resources

www.Quicken.com/products

www.youneedabudget.com

www.mint.com

www.everydollar.com

Budget and Expense Reduction Resources

www.magicjack.com

www.ooma.com

www.freedompop.com

www.netflix.com

www.hulu.com

www.sling.com

www.credit.org

Sales, Coupons and Clearance Resources

www.bbb.org (Better Business Bureau)

www.retailmenot.com

www.retale.com

www.offers.com

www.dealtaker.com

www.groupon.com

www.techdeals.com

www.travelcoupons.com

www.expedia.com

www.travelocity.com

www.kayak.com

www.trivago.com

www.hotels.com

www.ibotta.com

www.babycheapskate.com

www.aarp.org

www.aaa.com

www.clark.com

www.consumerreports.org

www.rakuten.com

www.joinhoney.com

www.camelcamelcamel.com

www.shopsavvy.com (download from Google Play Store or iTunes)

www.gasbuddy.com (download the app to find gas prices on-the-go)

Eating Well on a Budget Resources

www.localfarmers.org

www.5dollarmealplan.com

www.SmartSource.com

www.valpak.com/coupons/savings/groceries

www.coupons.com

www.ibotta.com

www.extremebargains.net/discount-grocery-store-directory/

Dressing Well on a Budget Resources

www.thredup.com

www.poshmark.com

www.swap.com

www.pinterest.com

Entertainment Free and Cheap Resources

Local chamber of commerce

www.nps.gov (National Park Service)

www.geocaching.com

www.volunteermatch.org

www.meetup.com

www.facebook.com/groups

If Ends Don't Meet Resources

www.fiverr.com

www.virtualassistants.com

www.upwork.com

www.ebay.com

www.letgo.com

www.etsy.com

www.mspa-na.org

www.shutterstock.com

www.roadie.com

flex.amazon.com

Getting Ahead and Staying Ahead Resources

www.bankrate.com

www.irs.gov/publications/p970/

www.clark.com/education/clarks-529-plan-guide/

www.savingforcollege.com

www.fafsa.ed.gov

www.napfa.org

The Next Level Resources

www.biggerpockets.com/guides

www.nomadlist.com/fire

www.salary.com

www.payscale.com

www.earlyretirementnow.com/safe-withdrawal-rate-series/

www.choosefi.com

Bonus - Travel Hacking Resources

www.creditkarma.com

www.google.com/flights

www.travel.choosefi.com

Living Below Your Means

About the Author

After suffering her own financial crisis, Jennifer Raschig has completely turned around the outlook for her future. She is now living a life of financial freedom. Armed with degrees in business and accounting, she currently provides financial advice to many others through her business, More Than Organizing (www.morethanorganizing.com).

www.ingramcontent.com/pod-product-compliance
Lightning Source LLC
Chambersburg PA
CBHW030937240526
45463CB00015B/250

*9 7 8 1 6 5 8 7 0 5 1 0 3 *